When in Ge DO AS THE GERMANS DO

The Clued-In Guide to German Life, Language, and Culture

Second Edition

Hyde Flippo

New York Chicago San Francisco Athens London Madrid Mexico City
Milan New Delhi Singapore Sydney Toronto

1 2 3 4 5 6 7 8 9 0   LCR   23 22 21 20 19 18

ISBN   978-1-260-12163-6
MHID   1-260-12163-1
e-ISBN   978-1-260-12164-3
e-MHID   1-260-12164-X

Illustrations by Fred Dolven
Photos, including cover photo, by Hyde Flippo
Map by Mapping Specialists

Contents

Test Yourself Quizlinks   1

Articles

Arts and Culture   9
Business and Economy   14
Celebrations and Holidays   19
Consumers and Shopping   27
Daily Life and Customs   33
Education   44
Entertainment   48
Food and Drink   52
Geography   59
Health and Fitness   66
History and Famous People   70
House and Home   77
Justice and Law Enforcement   84
Language   87
Media   93
Politics   96
Religion and Beliefs   103
Science and Technology   109
Social Issues and Attitudes   115
Transportation   124

Quizlink Answers   135

Map of Germany   136

Index   137

Test Yourself Quizlinks

When in Germany, do you know how to fit in by doing as the Germans do? How sensitive are you to German customs and traditions? And how aware are you of contemporary daily life and typical domestic routines of the German people?

The following multiple-choice questions will test how much you know about all aspects of German culture. There are 120 questions in all, each corresponding to a specific article within the book. To discover the answer and more information about the subject, follow the quizlink to the relevant article. Alternatively, you can check the answers listed at the back of the book.

Do as the Germans Do

1. When do Germans use a TAN generator? ▶14
   - (a) before vacationing in Mallorca
   - (b) while banking online
   - (c) after suffering a power outage

2. What usually happens on your birthday at work? ▶19
   - (a) colleagues play tricks on you
   - (b) you are given a cake and small gifts
   - (c) you are expected to provide cake and champagne

3. By what method do most German customers pay for online purchases? ▶32
   - (a) bank draft
   - (b) credit card
   - (c) online pay service

4. What is an appropriate topic to begin a business meeting? ▶35
   - (a) the weather
   - (b) family
   - (c) get straight down to business

5. Which of the following should you *not* address as *du*? ▶37
   - (a) a child
   - (b) a group of close friends
   - (c) a pet

6. What is the most correct way to attract the attention of a waitress? ▶38
   - (a) *"Fräulein!"*
   - (b) *"Frau!"*
   - (c) *"Frau"* plus her surname

7. What do most German men usually wear to work? ▶39
   - (a) a suit and tie
   - (b) jeans and sports coat
   - (c) shorts and t-shirt

8. If you need to relieve yourself, what should you *not* ask directions for? ▶40
   - (a) *das Badezimmer*
   - (b) *die Toilette*
   - (c) *das WC*

9. What should you generally do on entering a restaurant? ▶57
   - (a) wait to be seated
   - (b) ask a food server for a table
   - (c) find a table yourself

10. Where should you go to buy prescription medicine? ▶69
    - (a) *Apotheke*
    - (b) *Drogerie*
    - (c) *Supermarkt*

11. What should you recycle in the "Yellow Sack"? ▶80
    - (a) biodegradable waste
    - (b) packaging materials
    - (c) glass

12. What does a *"KEHRWOCHE"* sign outside your apartment oblige you to do for the week? ▶81
    - (a) cleaning duties
    - (b) deliver papers and mail
    - (c) put out recycling

TEST YOURSELF QUIZLINKS

13. In the event of an emergency in a public building, what sign should you look for? ▶87
    (a) "*AUSGANG*"   (b) "*EINSTIEG*"   (c) "*NOTAUSGANG*"

14. Where should you go to buy health foods? ▶88
    (a) *Evergreen*   (b) *Reformhaus*   (c) *Warenhaus*

Places

1. What appears on the reverse side of German coins smaller than 1 euro? ▶15
   (a) the Brandenburg Gate   (b) Neuschwanstein Castle   (c) Cologne Cathedral

2. Where is Germany's home for startups, "Silicon Allee," located? ▶17
   (a) Berlin   (b) Frankfurt   (c) Munich

3. All these construction projects have suffered delays and cost overruns, but which is the only one (as of 2018) to be completed? ▶18
   (a) Hamburg's Elbe   (b) Berlin's BER airport   (c) Stuttgart's S21 urban
       Philharmonic Hall   development

4. Link each of these three festivals to its region. ▶21
   (a) *Karneval*   (b) *Fastnacht*   (c) *Fasching*
   (i) Rhineland   (ii) Bavaria   (iii) Baden

5. What guidebook was the first to use the "Baedeker system" in 1839? ▶60
   (a) Baedeker Rhine   (b) Baedeker Paris   (c) Baedeker Venice

6. Where is the Bismarck Sea, a current-day reminder of a former German colony? ▶64
   (a) Kenya   (b) New Guinea   (c) Namibia

7. What Alpine city boasts the longest ski season in the Alps? ▶65
   (a) Garmisch   (b) Innsbruck   (c) Zermatt

8. The name of the famed 19th-century Prussian naturalist, Humboldt, was once proposed for what new U.S. state? ▶74
   (a) Nevada   (b) Oregon   (c) Utah

9. The new Reichstag opened in 1999, cementing the restoration of Berlin as the home of united German government. Who designed it? ▶96
   (a) Daniel Liebeskind   (b) I.M. Pei   (c) Norman Foster

10. In which region of Germany did the far right AfD party gain a majority in the 2017 election? ▶99
    (a) Baden-Württemberg   (b) Franconia   (c) Sachsen (Saxony)

11. In which city are both Mercedes and Porsche based? ▶124
    (a) Munich   (b) Stuttgart   (c) Wolfsburg

12. Which of these cities does not have a metro system? ▶128
    (a) Dresden   (b) Frankfurt am Main   (c) Stuttgart

People

1. Goethe's novel *Werther*, published in 1779, was credited with causing what phenomenon? ▶9
   (a) the South Sea Bubble   (b) popular uprisings   (c) rejected-lover suicides

2. To whom is Germany's oldest literary society dedicated? ▶10
   (a) Goethe   (b) Shakespeare   (c) Dante

3. Who traditionally brings Christmas gifts to children in southern Germany? ▶25
   (a) *Weihnachtsmann*   (b) *Christkind*   (c) *Krampus*

4. What saint gives his or her name to New Year's Eve? ▶26
   (a) Silvester   (b) Magdalena   (c) Elisabeth

5. Who or what is Ötzi? ▶61
   (a) a derogatory term for an East German   (b) an Alpine ice man   (c) a popular TV clown

6. Who first established a national health care insurance system in Germany? ▶66
   (a) Frederick the Great   (b) Otto von Bismarck   (c) Karl Adenauer

7. What was the true profession of the famed impostor called the Captain from Köpenick? ▶70
   (a) librarian   (b) cobbler   (c) chimney sweep

8. Bertha von Suttner was the first woman to win what? ▶71
   (a) an Academy award (Oscar)   (b) the Nobel Peace Prize   (c) Gold in three consecutive Olympics

9. Where was Albert Einstein working when he developed his theory of relativity? ▶75
   (a) a patent office in Bern   (b) a customs house in Munich   (c) a restaurant in Ulm

10. Which of the following statements is *not* true of German Chancellor Angela Merkel? ▶76
    (a) her father was a Lutheran pastor   (b) she excelled in school at Russian   (c) her second (and current) husband is a law professor

11. Who translated the first Germanic Bible? ▶105
    (a) Ulfilas   (b) Gutenberg   (c) Luther

12. Who designed Berlin's Jewish Museum? ▶107
    (a) Ludwig Mies van der Rohe   (b) Richard Rogers   (c) Daniel Libeskind

13. Who invented aspirin? ▶109
    (a) Friedrich Bayer   (b) Felix Hoffmann   (c) Gustav Aspirin

14. For what is Dr. Magnus Hirschfeld known? ▶122
    (a) founder of Zionism   (b) father of gay rights movement   (c) discoverer of a cure for syphilis

Organizations

1. What German–United States union ended in divorce in 2007? ▶16
   (a) Bayer & Pfeizer   (b) Daimler & Chrysler   (c) Steffi Graf & Andre Agassi

2. Which of these U.S. companies tried and failed in the German market? ▶30
   (a) Starbucks   (b) McDonald's   (c) Wal-Mart

3. Which of the following abbreviations is *not* a type of German corporation? ▶92
   (a) AG   (b) GmbH   (c) ZDF

TEST YOURSELF QUIZLINKS

4. In addition to a core political philosophy and an abbreviation or nickname, each of Germany's political parties has what? ▶100
   - (a) a mascot
   - (b) a color
   - (c) a flower

5. Members of what organization are barred from government jobs in Bavaria? ▶108
   - (a) Communist party
   - (b) Bündnis 90
   - (c) Church of Scientology

6. Which of these distinctive features applies to German telecommunications? ▶112
   - (a) a monopoly on land lines
   - (b) two country codes (for West and East)
   - (c) area codes of varying length

7. Compared with other countries, Internet access in Switzerland is particularly ... ▶114
   - (a) fast
   - (b) slow
   - (c) expensive

8. Austria's top billionaire, Didi Mateschitz, is the founder of what company? ▶116
   - (a) Red Bull (energy drinks)
   - (b) Spar (grocery stores)
   - (c) Swarovski (glass crystal)

Time

1. In what period are Karl May's popular novels set? ▶11
   - (a) Roman Empire
   - (b) Crusades
   - (c) Wild West

2. How are summer vacations in Germany staggered? ▶22
   - (a) by profession/industry
   - (b) by state
   - (c) by first letter of surname

3. *Martinstag* on November 11 celebrates Martin of Tours. What holy act did he perform? ▶23
   - (a) curing a leper
   - (b) clothing a beggar
   - (c) turning water into beer

4. Provided a parent or guardian is present, at what age may you legally consume beer or wine in public in Germany? ▶34
   - (a) 11
   - (b) 14
   - (c) 17

5. At what age must German students decide their type of secondary schooling? ▶45
   - (a) 10
   - (b) 12
   - (c) 13

6. Approximately when was Berlin founded? ▶62
   - (a) 150 B.C.
   - (b) A.D. 450
   - (c) A.D. 1200

7. When was the first official smoking ban instituted in Germany? ▶68
   - (a) 1941
   - (b) 1968
   - (c) 2007

8. What is celebrated on October 3? ▶72
   - (a) the founding of the Federal Republic
   - (b) German reunification
   - (c) the collapse of the Berlin Wall

9. What is the typical length of a long-term mortgage in Germany? ▶77
   - (a) 15 years
   - (b) 25 years
   - (c) 30 years

10. How long must German youths serve in the military? ▶98
    - (a) not compulsory
    - (b) 10 months
    - (c) 16 months

11. For how long must foreign adults live in Germany before they can apply for citizenship? ▶117
    (a) 3 years   (b) 8 years   (c) 15 years

12. When did Karl Kreile and Bodo Mende become Germany's first official same-sex married couple? ▶121
    (a) 1987   (b) 2003   (c) 2017

13. For how long can a non-German drive on a foreign license in Germany? ▶126
    (a) 6 months   (b) 12 months   (c) unlimited

Quantity

1. Which of the following is *not* measured in metric units? ▶42
   (a) apartment dimensions   (b) recipe ingredients   (c) tire size

2. Of Germany's 300 universities, approximately how many are private? ▶47
   (a) fewer than 5 percent   (b) 10 percent   (c) 20 percent

3. How many varieties of sausage are there? ▶53
   (a) 500   (b) 1,000   (c) 1,500

4. How much mineral water do Germans drink per person per year (for comparison: the British drink 36 liters)? ▶58
   (a) 65 liters   (b) 120 liters   (c) 175 liters

5. There are an estimated 25 million of these objects currently in Germany. What are they? ▶82
   (a) cuckoo clocks   (b) pairs of lederhosen   (c) garden gnomes

6. What is the largest ethnic minority living in Germany? ▶106
   (a) Hungarian   (b) Polish   (c) Turkish

7. How many inhabitants of Germany's population of 83 million are foreigners? ▶118
   (a) 12 million (14 percent)   (b) 19 million (22 percent)   (c) 26 million (31 percent)

8. How many penalty points result in the loss of a driver's license (drunk driving counts as 7 points)? ▶127
   (a) 8 points   (b) 12 points   (c) 18 points

9. How many classes of train travel does Germany offer? ▶129
   (a) only one standard class   (b) two   (c) three

Connections

1. To what U.S. city did the Bauhaus movement transfer? ▶12
   (a) Detroit   (b) Philadelphia   (c) Chicago

2. What is the Germanic ancestor of the Punxsutawney Phil groundhog? ▶20
   (a) a beaver   (b) a hedgehog   (c) a porcupine

3. Which of these items can you *not* usefully take to Germany? ▶33
   (a) your ATM card   (b) your mobile phone   (c) your electric alarm clock

4. What U.S. movie was based on German author Erich Kästner's tale *Das doppelte Lottchen*? ▶48
   (a) *Beauty and the Beast*   (b) *The Parent Trap*   (c) *Elf*

5. What designation applies to movies shown in the original language with German subtitles? ▶49
   (a) OV   (b) O-Ton   (c) OmU

6. How does a typical German washing machine compare with American models? ▶79
   (a) uses more water   (b) spins more slowly   (c) uses hotter water

7. What is Germany's rate of incarceration per 100,000 (for comparison, the U.S. rate is 666)? ▶84
   (a) 77   (b) 133   (c) 208

8. Germany's BKA can be compared to what American organization? ▶86
   (a) Federal Bureau of Investigation   (b) Internal Revenue Service   (c) National Rifle Association

9. How is the word *TV* pronounced in German? ▶89
   (a) TAY-VAY   (b) TEE-VEE   (c) TAY-FOW

10. Which of the following is not a German word? ▶91
    (a) *der Smoking*   (b) *das Lifting*   (c) *der Opening*

What's That?

1. What semi-legal feature of German cities are *Spätis*? ▶29
   (a) convenience stores   (b) unregistered cabs   (c) massage parlors

2. What is the unofficial division between north and south Germany called? ▶59
   (a) "The Currywurst Curtain"   (b) "The White-sausage Equator"   (c) "No-man's Länder"

3. What is this symbol: ẞ? ▶90
   (a) abbreviation for *Freizeit* (free time)   (b) symbol for airplane (*Flugzeug*)   (c) capitalized ß

4. What is a *GroKo*, German word of the year in 2013? ▶102
   (a) a political coalition   (b) an energy drink mixed with protein supplement   (c) Bundesliga antiracism in soccer movement

5. What is the origin of the *Jugendweihe* celebration? ▶103
   (a) Bavarian Catholicism   (b) North German Lutheranism   (c) East German Communism

6. What is *ein Handy*? ▶111
   (a) a mobile phone   (b) a personal organizer   (c) a sanitary wipe

7. What are Germany's crème de la crème elite known as? ▶115
   (a) "the upper 10,000"   (b) "the golden circle"   (c) "the blessed 1 percent"

Laws and Regulations

1. What does the German law, *das Ladenschlussgesetz*, concern? ▶28
   (a) recycling   (b) speed limits   (c) store closing hours

2. Which of these is a compulsory feature of the German educational system? ▶44
   (a) 13 years' education   (b) kindergarten   (c) religious education

3. What right to placement in a nearby kindergarten or child care is mandated by Federal law? ▶46
   (a) 2 hours daily from age 2   (b) half day from age 4   (c) full day from age 5

4. What does the *Reinheitsgebot*, the oldest consumer protection law in Germany, cover? ▶55
   (a) bread   (b) beer   (c) sausage

5. What home appliance is outlawed in Germany? ▶78
   (a) in-sink garbage disposal   (b) leaf blower   (c) home brew kit

6. For what is the *Rundfunkbeitrag* fee levied on each household? ▶93
   (a) garbage collection   (b) TV/radio license   (c) water and sewage

7. For what are German film ratings most likely to restrict a movie to "16 and up"? ▶94
   (a) sexual situations   (b) violence   (c) strong language

8. What tax is levied on almost all Germans but usually exempts foreign nationals? ▶104
   (a) national monument tax   (b) reconstruction tax   (c) church tax

9. What size apartment buildings are required by law to have elevators installed? ▶119
   (a) four-story and above   (b) six-story and above   (c) no legal requirement

10. Beate Uhse built a large chain of stores across Germany—in what business? ▶120
    (a) home improvement outlets   (b) sex shops   (c) test prep tutoring

11. Which of these industries was deregulated in 2012? ▶134
    (a) waste management   (b) long-distance buses   (c) telecommunications

Know What the Germans Know

1. Which tree is most commonly associated with Saint Barbara's Feast (Dec. 4)? ▶24
   (a) acacia   (b) birch   (c) cherry

2. What credit/debit card is most widely accepted in Germany? ▶27
   (a) Visa   (b) EC/Maestro   (c) Diner's

3. What is the main emergency number to call in Germany? ▶36
   (a) 007   (b) 112   (c) 999

4. Which of the following popular German bands is known for punk music? ▶51
   (a) Die toten Hosen   (b) Ich + Ich   (c) 2raumwohnung

TEST YOURSELF QUIZLINKS

5. Which of these grape varieties is a common source of German wines? ▶52
   (a) Shiraz (b) Sylvaner (c) Zinfandel

6. Which of these treatments is covered by German health insurance? ▶67
   (a) spa visits (b) liposuction (c) cosmetic plastic surgery

7. Which of these features is most commonly found in German apartments? ▶83
   (a) wall-to-wall carpeting (b) a lock on every internal door (c) central air conditioning

8. What are Schupo and Kripo? ▶85
   (a) TV talent show hosts (b) mascots for past German World Cup tournaments (c) divisions of state police force

9. Which publication is the most appropriate to buy for a highbrow colleague? ▶95
   (a) *Bild* (b) *Stern* (c) *Die Zeit*

10. Which type of spacecraft took the first German into orbit? ▶110
    (a) Apollo (b) space shuttle (c) Soyuz

11. Which of these is a feature of burial in Germany? ▶123
    (a) no cremation allowed (b) short-term rights to burial places (c) recycling of funeral caskets

12. What is the fastest train service in Germany? ▶130
    (a) EC (b) IC (c) ICE

13. On what type of transportation is a ticket from a *Fahrkartenautomaten* valid? ▶132
    (a) bus (b) metro and streetcar (c) all forms

Goethe's Bestseller: The Novel That Swept the World in the 1770s

As August 28, 1999, approached, Germany prepared to celebrate the 250th birthday of its best-known cultural icon: Johann Wolfgang von Goethe (1749–1832). It was to be a *"Goethe-Jahr,"* a commemorative year for the German author, poet, dramatist, philosopher, and scientist who continues to hold the undisputed crown as the preeminent symbol of German culture—at home and abroad—more than a century and a half after his death. Although his life and work have been examined, researched, and written about more than that of probably any other German figure in history, the *Goethe-Jahr* inspired even more Goethe frenzy in print, on the air, and on the Web.

Best known for the drama *Faust* and his other classic works of literature, Goethe also dabbled in popular literature. In 1774, he published a novel that became a worldwide bestseller, *Die Leiden des jungen Werthers* (*The Sorrows of Young Werther*). Things moved a little more slowly in those days, and it was three years after the American Revolution before the English translation appeared, in 1779. The first *Sturm und Drang* (storm and stress) novel, *Werther* was written as an exchange of letters between lovers. Its neurotic, egotistical, lovesick teenage central character spawned an 18th-century global rash of rejected-lover suicides similar to that in the novel.

The semiautobiographical *Werther* reflected Goethe's romantic suffering (the more accurate translation of the title's original *Leiden*) over Charlotte Buff in Wetzlar. Goethe even named the love interest in his work Charlotte (Lotte).

No head-in-the-clouds technophobe, Goethe displayed his convictions regarding social and technological progress, most notably in *Wilhelm Meisters Lehrjahre* (*Wilhelm Meister's Travels*), written in 1821–29.

Goethe the Man

Who was this man who provokes such extreme devotion—and criticism—from Germans and others? It's not an easy question to answer.

The "Gothic Shakespeare" was much more than that—a complex figure of numerous contrasts in many fields. In his long life and career (he died only months before his 84th birthday), Goethe the author and poet wrote a worldwide bestselling novel (*Die Leiden des jungen Werthers*, 1774) as well as a landmark of German and world literature—the poetic, deeply philosophical two-part drama *Faust* (Part I, 1808; Part II, 1832). Goethe the scientist and researcher wrote *Metamorphose der Pflanzen* (*The Metamorphosis of Plants*) in 1790 and *Farbenlehre* (*Theory of Color*) in 1805–10. His science might have been faulty (particularly in *Farbenlehre*) and his valid discoveries often made after others, but Goethe's writings on the history of science and his insight into the mental process and the problems of scientific inquiry command respect to this day. And Goethe the philosopher intertwined themes of religion and science in his poetic series titled *Gott und Welt* (*God and World*), published in 1827.

Related Web links: gutenberg.spiegel.de/autor/johann-wolfgang-von-goethe-205—Projekt Gutenberg, with many of Goethe's works online (G); dw-world.de—Deutsche Welle site (E, G)

Shakespeare in German: *Der Schwan vom Avon*

Strange as it may seem, the German Shakespeare Society (die Deutsche Shakespeare-Gesellschaft, DSG) is the world's oldest. Founded in 1864, on the occasion of the Bard's 300th birthday (*zum 300. Geburtstag vom Barden*), the society is headquartered in Weimar, a city that is also closely associated with the real "German Shakespeare," Johann Wolfgang von Goethe.

Divided by the Cold War and the Berlin Wall for three decades, Germany's oldest literary society successfully managed its own reunification in 1993. Each year in April, the month of Shakespeare's birth and death, the DSG sponsors its *Shakespeare-Tage* (Shakespeare Days), an international event that alternates locales between Weimar and Bochum, the former western headquarters. The society also promotes meetings, seminars, and research and publishes a booklike annual journal, *Das Shakespeare-Jahrbuch*, in English and German.

The German fascination with Shakespeare began in the early 1700s when English repertoire companies crossed the *Ärmelkanal* to perform the Bard's plays all across Germany and Europe. Translations of Shakespeare's words have become so much a part of the German language that Germans can be forgiven if they sometimes seem to forget that William Shakespeare was not Wilhelm Shakespeare. In fact, the Germans take a backseat to no one when it comes to honoring the greatest English poet of all time. They do so by performing and attending his plays (more performances are given each year than in Britain!), using his words and phrases, and joining Shakespeare clubs and associations. There's even a replica of the Globe Theatre in Neuss, not far from Düsseldorf. Each season in Neuss, the German Globe offers a program of Shakespeare productions—in both German and English.

As in the English-speaking world, Germans often fail to realize just how much of their vocabulary comes from Shakespeare. Then again, *was ist ein Name?* (what's in a name?). They would no doubt consider such concerns *viel Lärm um nichts* (much ado about nothing). Worrying about such things could be *der Anfang vom Ende* (the beginning of the end).

Over the years, many German literary figures have translated Shakespeare into the language of Goethe and Schiller. (Among other works, Goethe's "Götz von Berlichingen" shows Shakespeare's influence.) For many of the Bard's plays and sonnets it is possible to find several German versions that have been translated at different times by different poets. Ironically, this means that it is usually easier to read Shakespeare in German (if you're German) than in English! The English of Shakespeare's time is often foreign to modern ears, but the German translations tend to be in more modern German than the Elizabethan English of the originals.

Related Web links: shakespeare-gesell schaft.de—Deutsche Shakespeare-Gesellschaft (German Shakespeare Society) (E, G)

Cowboys and Indians—Not Necessarily in That Order

The German fascination with *Indianer* and the American Wild West often strikes Americans as odd, but it is a solid element of German culture. Although it is now a fading practice in the age of television and video games, almost every adult in the German-speaking world today read Karl May's tales of the West as a child. You may never have heard of Karl May (pronounced MY), but he is the German Zane Grey or Louis L'Amour (also popular authors in German translation). A series of Western films in the 1960s and '70s based on May's books helped promote the German fascination with the American West.

Karl May was born into poverty near Chemnitz in 1842. Though scorned by the literary establishment, at his death in 1912, May had become one of Germany's best-read authors. His adventure tales of people and places he had never seen became popular fare for Germany's young readers. Volumes 1–33 made up his so-called travel adventures. Among the most popular figures in May's many books were the Indian Winnetou and his paleface friend Old Surehand. (Germans and Europeans have always favored the Indians over the cowboys!) Some of May's works have been translated into other languages, but they are hard to find.

In recent years in Germany, there has been a trend toward counteracting the romantic picture of Native Americans that May's books helped create. One current website asks (in German): "Is your image of Indians still mostly influenced by Winnetou?" Another German site is sponsored by the Native American Association of Germany e.V., which tries to update the German and European view of Indians and publicize related events in Europe, including genuine powwows.

Nevertheless, to this day there are traditional Western and Indian clubs all across Germany, some with their own Wild West saloon and/or Western fort. German summer camps offer *Tipi-Dörfer*, or tepee villages. The popular *Karl-May Festspiele* ("pageants") scattered around Germany still draw visitors who want to be entertained by outdoor re-creations of the stories about Winnetou. The most famous of these pageants, in Bad Segeberg, featured the actress Elke Sommer during the 1999 season (June through August). Two other European stars who used to play Winnetou in the movies, Pierre Brice and Gojko Mitic, were on hand for the production called *"Halbblut"* (Half-Breed), based on Karl May stories. One such pageant announced that attendance for 1999 was above the previous year. It seems the German love of the romantic Indian legend continues.

Related Web links: karl-may-gesellschaft.de—Karl-May-Gesellschaft (KM Society, KMG) presents the life and work of the author (G); karl-may-gesellschaft.de/index.php?seite=texts-by-karl-may&sprache=fremdsprachen—KMG, some of Karl May's works in English (E); karl-may-museum.de—Karl May Museum, near Dresden (G);

Bauhaus: From Gropius to Jahn

The Bauhaus connection spans over many decades. What links the cities of Dessau and Chicago, and connects the architects Walter Gropius, Ludwig Mies van der Rohe, and Helmut Jahn (the latter born more than half a century after Gropius and Mies van der Rohe)? The Bauhaus is the link.

The "house of building" design movement that originated in Germany around the beginning of the 1920s continues to exert an enormous influence on international architecture and design. Although the Bauhaus and its influences have as many detractors as proponents, there is no denying the movement's significant impact on structures as diverse as skyscrapers and teapots.

The Bauhaus (1919–33) is inseparable from its founder, German architect Walter Gropius (1883–1969). The famous school of art and industrial design (architecture was not officially added until 1927) was first established in Weimar. Officially known as the Staatliches Bauhaus Weimar, the school remained there until local resistance and financial difficulties forced a move to Dessau in 1925. Soon the Bauhaus had attracted an impressive cadre of artists and architects, including Paul Klee, Wassily Kandinsky, Lyonel Feininger, and Ludwig Mies van der Rohe.

Gropius (along with several other soon-to-be famous architects) worked for a time in the Berlin offices of German architect Peter Behrens (1868–1940) and was greatly influenced by him, particularly while working on Behrens's projects for the huge German electrical concern AEG.

As with most other things German, the Bauhaus also has its connection with the "German past" and the Nazis. With the advent of the Hitler regime, Gropius and his "decadent" school of design became unwelcome anywhere in Germany. After a brief move to Berlin, the Bauhaus was shut down in 1933. The "New Bauhaus" (later the Institute of Design) was reestablished in the New World in Chicago by the artist Laszlo Maholy-Nagy in 1937. At the same time, Gropius went to Harvard University and was soon appointed chair of the School of Architecture. He became a U.S. citizen in 1944 and remained at Harvard until his retirement in 1952. Gropius was active in The Architects Collaborative design firm, founded in 1946, until his death in 1969.

In 1938, Bauhaus protégé Ludwig Mies van der Rohe (1886–1969) became the head of what was later known as the Illinois Institute of Technology (IIT) in Chicago and designed its brand-new campus. Almost three decades later, in 1966, Helmut Jahn (born in 1940) began his graduate studies in architecture at IIT. In 1981, Jahn became a principal in the Chicago architectural firm of Murphy/Jahn. That same year, Jahn, like Gropius before him, became a professor of architecture at Harvard. Today the Nuremberg-born Jahn is a renowned international architect working on projects in Germany, the United States, and all over the world.

Related Web links: bauhaus.de—Bauhaus-Archiv, Berlin, a good site with biographies of all the main figures (G);

(E); **iit.edu**—Illinois Institute of Technology, see College of Architecture (E); **archinform.de/arch/277.htm**—Helmut Jahn Projects (E, G); **skyscrapercenter.com/city/frankfurt-am-main**—skyscrapers in Frankfurt am Main ("Mainhattan") (E, G)

The roof of the Sony Center on Berlin's Potsdamer Platz. German architect Helmut Jahn designed this complex and the neighboring 26-story BahnTower, both completed in 2000.

Banks and *Sparkassen*

Banking in the German-speaking world has a long tradition, going back to the 14th century and the banklike dealings of the north German Hanseatic League (*Hansa*). In the 15th and 16th centuries, the Augsburg-based Fugger moneylending and commercial dynasty held kings and kaisers (emperors) in its debt. Later, the House of Rothschild, based in Frankfurt am Main, carried on the far-reaching German banking tradition in the 19th century.

German banks today can be roughly divided into six categories:

1. Large commercial banks (Deutsche Bank, Commerzbank, etc.)
2. Government-owned state and regional wholesale banks (*Landesbanken*)
3. Savings banks (*Sparkassen*)
4. Smaller but ubiquitous cooperative credit banks (*Raiffeisenbanken, Volksbanken*)
5. The privatized postal savings bank system (Postbank AG)*
6. Online-only banks with smartphone apps and no physical presence

For travelers and those planning to live and work in German-speaking Europe today, an important word to learn is *Geldautomat*, German for ATM. Because Germans still prefer to use cash for everyday purchases, expats and tourists alike need to be prepared to pay with euro notes and coins. As you will read on p. 27, credit and debit cards are used far less often in Germany than in North America and many other countries. Having a German bank account will give you ATM access to cash, as well as get you the EC debit card that is often used for store purchases, even at places that don't accept credit cards.

Online banking is now as common in Germany as it is elsewhere, but with a few minor twists. The most important of these is the TAN, or transaction authentication number. A TAN is a six-digit, one-time password used as a second level of security, a type of two-factor authentication used in addition to a PIN or password. Bank customers used to receive a printed list of TAN codes. Nowadays they get a small electronic device called a "TAN generator." Some TAN generators require the insertion of your bank chip card in order to work. You hold it up to the computer screen during a transaction, and it generates a one-time code automatically. As you might suspect, it's a bit of a hassle, but it is very secure, something Germans value highly.

Some German banks are only online "Direktbanken," having no local branches; these include N26, DKB, and comdirect (the online division of Commerzbank). Comdirect is the only online bank in Germany that does not require that you have an address in Austria or Germany. To open a direct-bank account you have to use an online identity verification service (varies by bank) before completing your sign-up process. For N26, you use their phone/tablet app.

Deutsche Bank took over Postbank in 2010, although they have remained separately run entities.

Related Web links: n26.com, dkb.de, comdirect.de, deutschepost.de—banks and services; deutscheskonto .org/en/open-dkb-bank-account/—directions for opening a DKB online account (E)

€ for Euro: Germany and the Euro Zone

It is easy to forget just how nervous the introduction of brand new euro notes and coins in January 2002 made Germans. Even though the European Central Bank—the EU's "Fed"—had been located in Frankfurt ("Bankfurt") as part of the effort to persuade Germans to give up their mighty *Deutsche Mark* (DM), the euro (€) had been little more than an abstract concept since its birth as a cashless currency in 11 countries on January 1, 1999. In a nation that had experienced hyperinflation and worthless money in the 1920s, and the collapse of the *Reichsmark* after World War II, the untested euro was yet another cause for German angst.

Although former German chancellor (Oct. 1982–Oct. 1998) Helmut Kohl and his government were enthusiastic backers of both the European Union and the euro, average Germans had never displayed great enthusiasm for the EU's answer to the U.S. dollar. Public polls prior to the advent of the euro indicated that almost two-thirds of Germans had reservations about the loss of their familiar marks.

Austrians were also reluctant to adopt the euro, but at least they could take comfort in the fact that the colorful new euro banknotes were designed by Robert Kalina of the Austrian National Bank. (The coin designs were done by a Belgian.) Another German-speaking nation, Switzerland, is not an EU member and continues to use its Swiss franc (CHF).

The new euro bills and coins first went into circulation in January 2002 in a dozen European countries, including Austria and Germany. Although not all 28 European Union nations use the euro today, the euro zone gradually expanded over the years. In January 2015, Lithuania became the 19th country to adopt the common European currency.

The front (obverse, heads) side of euro coins is the same in all countries, but the reverse (tails) side is unique to each country. The German 10-, 20-, and 50-cent coins, for example, feature the Brandenburg Gate. Euro coins are minted in the following denominations: 1, 2, 5, 10, 20, 50 cent; 1- and 2-euro coins.

Euro notes have the same design in all countries, but unlike U.S. dollar bills, euro banknotes vary in size according to the denomination. The 5-euro bill is the lowest paper denomination and the smallest size. As the paper notes progress in amount— 5, 10, 20, 50, 100, 200, 500—they also increase in size. This makes it possible for blind people to feel the different sizes and denominations. As an anti–money-laundering step, the 500-euro note was scheduled to be phased out by the end of 2018. Existing 500s will still be legal tender, but no new 500-euro notes will be printed. The 200-euro note will then be the highest euro denomination.

Related Web links: german-way.com/travel-and-tourism/banks-money/the-euro/ Germany and the euro german-way.com/travel-and-tourism/banks-money/the-euro/euro-timeline/—Euro timeline (E), ecb.europa.eu/ecb/html/index.en.html—ECB, europa.eu/european-union/about-eu/money/euro_en—Euro and the EU (E)

German Brands and Multinational Corporations

Many German companies and products are household names all over the world. Few people anywhere would fail to recognize these German brands: Adidas, Audi, Bayer, BMW, Lufthansa, Mercedes (Daimler), Nivea, SAP, Siemens, and Volkswagen. The German bargain grocery chains Aldi and Lidl are now expanding in Europe and North America. Less well known is the German publishing and media company known as Bertelsmann. Headquartered in the small town of Gütersloh in North Rhine-Westphalia, this privately held multinational firm is one of the world's largest mass media companies. Among other entities, Bertelsmann owns Penguin Random House in the United States, and Luxembourg-based RTL Group, which operates radio and TV broadcasters in ten European countries, including RTL and VOX in Germany. Besides publishing firms in Germany and the United Kingdom, Stuttgart-based Holtzbrinck Publishing Group owns Macmillan (Henry Holt; Farrar, Straus and Giroux; St. Martin's Press, and other imprints) in the United States.

Not all German–American commercial ventures have gone according to plan. (See "Walmart's German Lesson" on p. 30.) From 1998 to 2007, DaimlerChrysler AG was the name of the new company formed by the $36 billion merger of two automakers, German Daimler-Benz and American Chrysler. Dubbed a "merger of equals," it was anything but. Not long after the merger, some wags told a joke that asked: How do you pronounce "Daimler-Chrysler" in German? Answer: The "Chrysler" part is silent.

Soon there was a major culture clash between the risk-averse Germans in Stuttgart and the more seat-of-the-pants Americans in Auburn Hills, Michigan. Planned synergies never fell into place. In 2000, DaimlerChrysler CEO Jürgen Schrempp admitted in a German interview that the German side never viewed the merger as one of equals. Chrysler was simply a subsidiary of the German company. In fact the two companies were never truly merged. Mistakes were made and lawsuits were filed. The divorce came in 2007.

Today, Chrysler is part of Fiat Chrysler Automobiles N.V. (FCA, since 2014), the world's eighth largest auto manufacturer, and the Italian–American joint venture seems to work much better than the German–American one did. Daimler AG is now ranked 13th for cars, but first for trucks and commercial vehicles.

In the world of finance, some of the world's best-known names are German. Allianz, with headquarters in Munich, is the world's largest insurance and financial services company, with a 2016 revenue of over 122 billion euros. Deutsche Bank has its twin towers headquarters in Frankfurt am Main. Founded in 1870, Deutsche Bank is now a global banking and financial services company, the 16th largest bank in the world by total assets (in 2017), with over 100,000 employees in 70 countries.

Related Web links: global.handelsblatt.com——German business news (E)

"Silicon Allee": The Internet and Tech Startups in Germany

Although Berlin's tech scene began around 2007, the term "Silicon Allee" arose in 2011 as a clever wordplay on New York City's "Silicon Alley," which itself is a play on "Silicon Valley." German tech startup centers exists in Cologne, Frankfurt, Hamburg, Munich, and other German locations, but Berlin's *Silicon Allee* ("Silicon Boulevard") is perhaps the best known. Berlin is the undisputed capital of Germany's startup scene. Home to Sound-Cloud, Wunderlist, Rocket Internet, and other notable tech firms, Berlin is the second largest startup hub in Europe, behind only London.

But the European Union has a tech funding problem, starting with venture capital being split up among the EU's 28 nations. Europe has long been a leader in scientific research, but it falls down on the D part of R&D, development. Skype was invented by a Dane, a Swede, and some Estonians in Tallinn, Estonia, in 2003. But international success came only after two American firms swooped in and invested billions in Skype: eBay ($2.6 billion) in 2005 and Microsoft ($8.5 billion) in 2011. Skype is still a Microsoft product, but the division's headquarters are in Luxembourg, with most of the development team and less than half of Skype's employees still working in Tallinn and Tartu, Estonia.

Silicon Allee is not a single geographic location. It's spread around Berlin, from the once-poor district of Kreuzberg, the now trendy Prenzlauer Berg, to central Mitte. The Factory's multiuse building, a former brewery, opened in Mitte in 2016 and backs up to where the Berlin Wall used to stand.

The startup space provider now competes with WeWork. Soon it also will go up against Google's new Berlin campus in Kreuzberg. But the Factory is noted for its innovative sessions and meetings designed to encourage even more tech development in Berlin and Germany as a whole.

Germany also has long been home to large, established tech companies such as the homegrown enterprise software firm SAP, headquartered in remote Walldorf, but with offices also in Berlin. SAP, founded in 1972, now has its own $35 million tech startup fund.

Another Berlin-based startup is the language-learning software firm Babbel, founded in 2007. Today Babbel (run by Lesson Nine GmbH) has about 450 employees in Berlin and New York City. The name "Babbel" comes from the Hessian dialect verb *babbeln*, to chat. It's also related to English "babble" and is a pun on the biblical Tower of Babel.

Although it is not a tech firm, the meal-kit service HelloFresh is Berlin-based and worked with Rocket Internet to expand. HelloFresh now serves the United States, the United Kingdom, the Netherlands, Austria, Australia, Belgium, Germany, and Switzerland. In May 2017, they added a wine club, HelloFresh Wine, in the United States.

Related Web link: www.hellofreshgroup.com/contact-us/ (HelloFresh countries)

German Efficiency?

Germans have a reputation for efficiency. However, even Germans have been heard to say: "If you want German efficiency, go to Switzerland." The worst German efficiency failures appear in major projects, ranging from Berlin's white elephant BER airport to Stuttgart's controversial rail project.

The new Berlin Brandenburg Willy Brandt Airport (BER) was scheduled to open on June 2, 2012—some 2 years after its planned 2010 debut. The grand opening was announced and set to go. Airlines were already selling tickets that displayed BER as the arrival or departure airport. The city's old Tegel (TXL) airport was set to close and move all operations to BER.

And then it happened. To everyone's amazement, it was announced that because of problems with the terminal's emergency smoke ventilation system, the opening would once again be delayed. Soon it was obvious there were many other defects and that management of the project was in chaos. Mayor Klaus Wowereit and his fellow politician BER board members seemed to be clueless. Five years later, in 2017, Wowereit was long gone, but incompetence still reigned after a series of "top managers" had tried and failed to get the airport open. Berliners have given up hope that BER will ever open, while TXL, opened in the early 1970s, struggles to serve a volume of passengers that it was never designed to handle. A promised opening in 2019 or 2020 leaves most people unconvinced. This is all the more irritating when you learn that Munich opened its brand new MUC airport on time and on budget in 1992.

Hamburg's new Elbe Philharmonic Hall is another example. Like BER, the concert hall was originally scheduled to open in 2010. Unlike BER, it finally did open in January 2017, but not before the structure's cost had risen more than 10 times over the original estimate of 77 million euros. But the *Elbphilharmonie*, as it's called in German, is already popular with locals and tourists alike.

Stuttgart 21 (S21) is a controversial, complex railway and urban development project. At its core is a renovated Stuttgart *Hauptbahnhof*, with 35 miles of new railways, including some 19 miles of tunnels and 16 miles of high-speed rail lines, plus improved airport connections. Almost from the start, the project has been beset by cost overruns, massive protests, and numerous delays.

Jointly funded by Deutsche Bahn, the federal government, the state of Baden-Württemberg, and the city of Stuttgart, construction on the S21 project began in February 2010, following extensive studies over more than a decade. Originally estimated at 2.45 billion euros, by early 2018 the cost had reached 8.2 billion euros (a federal cost projection said 10 billion euros) and the projected completion date was moved to 2021.

Related Web links: **berlin-airport.de/en**—site for Berlin's operational airports (E), **elbphilharmonie.de/en/** —Hamburg's philharmonic hall (E), **railway-technology.com/ projects/stuttgart21/**—status of S21 development (E)

Happy Birthday? *Alles Gute zum Geburtstag*!

If you thought that birthdays are celebrated pretty much the same all over the world, you'd be wrong. One of the best examples of a custom being turned upside down is the way German speakers celebrate birthdays. When you find out how this works, you may want to keep your own *Geburtstag* a top secret.

In sharp contrast to the procedure in English-speaking countries, the birthday boy or girl (*Geburtstagskind*) in Austria, Germany, or Switzerland is expected to put on the party, provide the cake, and pay for the drinks! It is the one having the birthday who treats friends and family to the celebration, not the other way around.

It is not unusual for German parents to give their son or daughter 50 euros or more to help finance a birthday bash for friends at a local restaurant. The poor birthday boy or girl often spends most of the days leading up to the party slaving over preparations, sometimes even baking the cake and working on the party decorations.

Adults at work are expected to offer cake or some other treat to coworkers. Usually a glass of champagne (*Sekt*) or other bubbly refreshment is also expected by fellow employees. And the older you are, the bigger the birthday bash is expected to be. If word leaks out that someone has a birthday, a crowd of friends and acquaintances (some the birthday person may never have seen before!) will soon gather for the customary treats. Oh, and one more thing. Never wish a German-speaking person a happy birthday before the actual birthday date! Doing so is considered bad luck.

Horoskop: What's your sign (*Zeichen*)?

The German *Tierkreiszeichen* (signs of the zodiac) reflect the animal or person associated with each sign: *Stier* (Taurus) is the bull, *Zwillinge* (Gemini) is the twins, and so forth.

In the following list, dates are shown in German format (e.g., 22.12–19.1 means December 22–January 19).

Steinbock (Capricorn): 22.12–19.1

Wassermann (Aquarius): 20.1–18.2

Fische (Pisces): 19.2–20.3

Widder (Aries): 21.3–20.4

Stier (Taurus): 21.4–20.5

Zwillinge (Gemini): 21.5–20.6

Krebs (Cancer): 21.6–22.7

Löwe (Leo): 23.7–22.8

Jungfrau (Virgo): 23.8–22.9

Waage (Libra): 23.9–22.10

Skorpion (Scorpio): 23.10–21.11

Schütze (Sagittarius): 22.11–21.12

Related Web link: thoughtco.com/signs-of-the-zodiac-in-german-4069391—the zodiac in German (E)

Groundhog Day: *Mariä Lichtmess*/Candlemas

February 2, *Mariä Lichtmess*—or Candlemas—was an official holiday in Germany until 1912. The day has also been known as *Mariä Reinigung, das Fest der Darstellung des Herrn*, and *Mariä Kerzenweihe*. The latter name (*Kerze* means "candle") is related to the English "Candlemas," with its tradition of blessing both sacred and household candles on February 2.

The American observance of Groundhog Day has its roots in this February holiday. At least as early as the 1840s, German immigrants in Pennsylvania had introduced the tradition of weather prediction that was associated with the hedgehog (*Igel*) in their homeland. Since there were no hedgehogs in the region, the Pennsylvania Germans adopted the indigenous woodchuck (a name derived from an Algonquian word), also known as the groundhog. The town of Punxsutawney has played up the custom over the years and managed to turn itself into the center of the annual Groundhog Day, particularly after the 1993 movie starring Bill Murray and Andie MacDowell. (In German the *Groundhog Day* film is called *Und täglich grüßt das Murmeltier*, which means "And daily the marmot [*Marmot monax*, groundhog] says hello.") Every year on February 2, people gather to wait to see whether a groundhog known as "Punxsutawney Phil" will see his shadow after he emerges from his burrow. If he does, the tradition says that there will be six more weeks of winter. (Unfortunately, Phil has a rather disappointing 39 percent rate of accuracy for his predictions.)

A similar German legend is connected with Saint Swithin's Day (*Siebenschläfer*, June 27), for which tradition says that if it rains on that day, it will rain for the next seven weeks. But the *Siebenschläfer* is a dormouse, not a hedgehog.

Related Web link: groundhog.org—the Official Punxsutawney Groundhog Club, for origins of the tradition, see History (E)

Die fünfte Jahreszeit: The Fifth Season

Germans call the pre-Lenten carnival season *die närrische Saison* (the foolish season) or *die fünfte Jahreszeit* (the fifth season). Except for Munich's Oktoberfest, it is the one time of year when many normally staid Germans (and Austrians and Swiss) loosen up and go a little crazy. *Fastnacht*, or *Karneval*, is a "movable feast" (*ein beweglicher Festtag*) that depends on the date of Easter (*Ostern*). The official start of the *Fasching* season is either January 7 (the day after Epiphany, *Dreikönige*) or the 11th day of the 11th month (*Elfter im Elften*, November 11), depending on the region. That gives the carnival guilds (*Zünfte*) three to four months to organize each year's events (balls, parades, royalty) leading up to the big bash the week before Ash Wednesday (*Aschermittwoch*), when the Lenten season (*die Fastenzeit*) begins.

Carnival in Rio is probably the world's most famous. In the United States, New Orleans is well known for Mardi Gras. While it is one of a few cities in the United States with a carnival celebration, close to all of the Catholic regions and cities across the German-speaking world, as well as the rest of Europe celebrate Mardi Gras in a big way. Only a few Protestant areas in northern and eastern Germany also observe *Karneval*. Some of Germany's best-known celebrations are held in Cologne, Mainz, Munich, and Rottweil. Germanic carnival celebrations vary from region to region, sometimes even taking place at different times. (The *Fasnacht* event in Basel, Switzerland, happens a week after most other carnivals.)

Carnival, or Mardi Gras, goes by many names in German, depending on the region and dialect—*Karneval* (Rhineland), *Fasching* (Austria, Bavaria), *Fastnacht* (Baden, Switzerland), *Fosnat* (Franconia), or *Fasnet* (Swabia). Whether it's *Fasching* or *Karneval*, it's a time to let off steam and live it up before the Lenten period that once called for fasting (*die Fastenzeit*). It is this fasting tradition that gave the celebration its *Fastnacht* name (night before fasting). In the 15th and 16th centuries, amusing plays known as *Fastnachtspiele* were performed during the pre-Lenten season. Today there are elaborate parades (*Umzüge*) in all the large and small communities where *Fasching* is celebrated. Floats and marchers displaying large caricature heads often lampoon regional and national politicians. Another part of the celebration involves carnival royalty (princes, princesses) and a sort of "counter-government" during the season. The Rhineland *Rosenmontagumzug* is an event broadcast each year on German television, much like the Macy's Thanksgiving parade in New York.

Fastnacht/Karneval

The word *Fastnacht* is related to the Germanic word *fasten* (to fast; abstain from eating). *Karneval* is related to the Latin *carnem levare* (to remove meat).

Related Web links: karneval.de—Cologne Karneval (E, G); **mainzer-fastnacht.de**—Mainz Fastnacht (G)

Summer Vacation and *Reisewellen*

The Germans have a word for it: *Sommerferienregelung*. The logical German practice of "summer vacation regulation" staggers the start of the annual summer break season among all of the 16 states (*Bundesländer*) and is supposed to avoid the chaos that would ensue if every state ended school for the summer on the same day. Remember, Germany is about the same size as the U.S. state of Montana, but it is much more densely populated. In theory at least, Germany's coordinated national vacation schedule means that all 82 million Germans don't hit the road on the same day, heading out for their sacred summer vacation in Austria, France, Italy, Scandinavia, or elsewhere.

In 2018, for instance, students in Berlin leave their books behind for summer on July 5 and return to school on August 17. Two years later, in 2020, Berlin schools close for the summer on June 25, returning to school on August 7. In the state of Bavaria for 2018, students get out on July 5 and return on September 10. In 2020 Bavaria's schools will have *Sommerferien* from July 27 to September 7. Similar staggered dates are arranged geographically to spread out the dates across Germany for the typical five weeks of freedom students get for their summer break that ends in August or September. You can find the dates for any school holiday in Germany far in advance for any year online at schulferien.org.

In reality, despite the varied vacation dates, in areas where the vacation period has begun, the highways and autobahns are no place for people with claustrophobia, as each wave (*Reisewelle*) of summer vacationers creates a series of *Staus*, or traffic jams, that can spread out for kilometers and kilometers.

Although there are no longer any border formalities on the German–Austrian border, traffic tends to clog up on many popular routes, including the Brenner Pass autobahn and stretches around and between Salzburg and Vienna.

> **Related Web link: schulferien.org**—school vacation dates for Germany (G)

So-called "beach baskets" (*Strandkörbe*) await rental at a German Baltic beach.

Halloween and *Martinstag*

Halloween isn't really a German holiday, but it has become one in recent decades. Its growing popularity since the 1990s, with help from Hollywood and television, is probably due to the way it combines elements of the German version of Mardi Gras (*Fasching/Karneval*) and *Martinstag*, with its lantern processions honoring St. Martin of Tours. "Trick or treat" becomes *Süßes oder Saures* in German (roughly "sweets or trouble"), but in Germany Halloween is often more for partying adults than children.

Halloween jack-o'-lanterns also fit in nicely with traditional fall pumpkin and gourd festivals long celebrated in parts of Austria and Germany. The region around Retz, Austria, not far from Vienna, holds an annual Halloween and *Kürbis* (pumpkin) festival, complete with a Halloween pageant and pumpkin carving.

In early October, plastic pumpkins, masks, costumes, and other Halloween items appear in German department stores and other shops. Hamburg has one of Germany's best-known Halloween stores, the Horror Shop (also online), which also sells Christmas, *Karneval*, and other costumes.

Not everyone in Germany has welcomed the invasion of a North American observance imported from Europe to the New World by Irish Catholic immigrants. Unfortunately, Halloween coincides with *Reformationstag*, the date when many Germans commemorate the Protestant Reformation that began on October 31, 1517, when Martin Luther allegedly nailed his 95 Theses to a church door in Wittenberg. Although Halloween (All Hallows' Eve) is part of the Western Christian observance of Allhallowtide, the three days dedicated to remembering the dead (October 31– November 2). Halloween's supposed pagan, Celtic/Anglo-Saxon roots caused it to be shunned by religious people, but today the pagan connection is increasingly doubtful. More enlightened church people have accepted Halloween as part of the Christian tradition.

Not long after Halloween, on November 11, a more traditional German holiday shares several elements with the trick-or-treat festival. St. Martin's Day (*Martini* in Austria) is related to Martin of Tours, a Roman soldier born around 316 C.E., who, according to legend, on a cold winter day gave half of his robe to a beggar. The incident led Martin to change his life by becoming a Christian. Three days after his death in 397, Martin was buried in the French town of Tours on November 11. Today, children singing "Ich gehe mit meiner Laterne…" ("I walk with my lantern…") and carrying handmade candle-lit paper lanterns, march in a procession, sometimes accompanied by a rider on a white horse representing St. Martin. In some regions, there may also be a St. Martin's bonfire. Celebrated in other parts of northern Europe, *Martinstag* is also observed in Protestant regions of Germany, including Berlin, where it takes on a more secular aspect in local elementary schools.

Related Web link: horror-shop.com/kostueme/ halloween-kostueme—Horror Shop, Hamburg (G)

Barbarazweig—A December Custom

The patron saint of miners, artillerymen, and firefighters, *die heilige Barbara* (Saint Barbara, d. 306) has lent her name to a Germanic Christmas custom that has its roots (literally) in the pre-Christian era. The legend of her martyrdom, on the other hand, seems to have originated around the seventh century. Officially, she is one of the 14 auxiliary saints, or holy helpers.

December 4 is the feast day of Saint Barbara, and this date plays a key role in the custom that bears the name of this virgin martyr. According to legend, Barbara lived in Asia Minor in what is today Turkey. Her father was the pagan emperor Dioscorus, a suspicious, untrusting fellow who persecuted Christians and kept his daughter a virgin by locking her up in a tower whenever he was away.

One day when he returned home, Dioscorus noticed that the tower where he kept his daughter under lock and key now had three windows instead of two. Puzzled, he asked her why she had added a window in his absence. Barbara then made the mistake of confessing that she had become a Christian and the three windows represented the trinity of her new faith. Incensed, her father demanded that she renounce this heresy. After some time had passed and she still stubbornly refused to deny her new religion, he commanded that she be tortured and beheaded. The legend further says that immediately following this gruesome event, Dioscorus was struck dead by lightning, which may explain why Saint Barbara is often invoked during thunderstorms.

Another important element of the *Barbara-Legende* concerns her imprisonment, which led (according to legend) to the Christmas custom that bears her name. Depressed and alone in her cell, Barbara found a dried cherry tree branch, which she moistened daily with a few drops from her drinking water. She was greatly consoled by the beautiful cherry blossoms that appeared just days before her impending execution.

The Barbara Branch Custom

Traditionally in the German-speaking countries, particularly in Austria and the Catholic regions of Germany, a small cherry branch is cut on December 4, *Barbaratag* (Saint Barbara's Day). Sometimes a twig from another flowering plant or tree—apple, forsythia, plum, lilac, or similar blossoms—may be used, but the cherry tree is most customary and authentic.

The cherry branch (*Kirschzweig*) or other cutting is then placed in water and kept in a warm room. If all goes well, on Christmas Day the twig will display blossoms. If it blooms precisely on December 25, this is regarded as a particularly good sign for the future.

Advent and Christmas in German-Speaking Europe

Germany and neighboring Austria and Switzerland really know how to celebrate Christmas! North Americans and Britons will recognize many of the Yuletide traditions they witness in German-speaking Europe, mostly because so many of them originated there.

Christmas tree? From Germany. The "Silent Night" carol? From Austria. Santa Claus/Father Christmas, aka Kris Kringle? From Germany, but it's complicated. Advent calendar? From Germany. Marzipan? Lübeck, Germany (Hanseatic League via Persia/Turkey, Italy, or Spain). Decorative nutcrackers? Germany (*Erzgebirge*). Glass tree ornaments? Germany. The glass pickle Christmas tree ornament? Nope. A myth created in the United States.

There are some Christmas traditions that are either unique to Germany or more widespread there. One example: the Christmas market. Although you can find good imitations in many other places, no one does a *Weihnachtsmarkt* like the Germans do. (*Glühwein*, hot mulled wine, is a key factor.) Advent, the 4 weeks leading up to Christmas, is not unknown in the United States, but in Germany it is a key part of the holidays, with many families lighting a candle on the Advent wreath each week. Christmas Eve is when families gather around the tree to exchange gifts. Santa (*der Weihnachtsmann*) doesn't come down the chimney, as there is usually no chimney.

But the Germans have some Christmas traditions that are found only in Germany and neighboring lands. These include *Barbarazweig* (Dec. 4), *Nikolaustag* (Dec. 6), and a 2-day Christmas observance (Dec. 25 and 26, as with Boxing Day in the United Kingdom). January 6 is *Dreikönigstag* (Three Kings/Epiphany) when the *Sternsinger* ("star singers") finish caroling door-to-door to raise funds for nationwide charities in Germany, Austria, and Belgium. A related custom involves writing a blessing above the main door of the home. For instance if the year is 2018, the inscription would be "20 * C + M + B * 18." The "CMB" initials refer to the Latin phrase *Christus mansionem benedicat* (may Christ bless this house), but most people interpret CMB as the names of the Three Wise Men (Caspar, Melchior, Balthasar).

Who brings German children Christmas gifts? That depends on where you live in Germany. In southern Germany, Catholic Bavaria, and Austria, it's the *Christkind*, an angelic, childlike figure, usually represented by a blonde girl. In northern, mostly Protestant, Germany, it's the *Weihnachtsmann* (Father Christmas). Ironically, the *Christkind* was created by the Protestant Luther to replace the Catholic St. Nicholas. But wait, there's more! In Catholic regions, kids also leave their shoes out on the night of Dec. 5 for Nikolaus, who fills them with small gifts for St. Nicholas Day on Dec. 6. This is also when Krampus, a menacing devil-like figure, appears in Alpine regions, scaring children—and even adults—out of their wits in a nighttime procession called a *Krampuslauf*.

Related Web links: german-way.com/history-and-culture/holidays-and-celebrations/christmas/a-to-z-guide-to-christmas-traditions/ A-to-Z Guide to Christmas Traditions; seriouseats.com/2010/12/marzipan-history-what-is-it-almonds.html Marzipan History

Silvester—New Year's Eve

Of all the German New Year's customs, surely "Dinner for One" has to be the oddest. For more than two decades, not a single New Year's Eve has gone by without this 15-minute English-language television sketch being broadcast all across Germany. A German New Year's Eve just doesn't seem right without hearing the lines known to almost any living German: "'Same procedure as last year, Madam?' 'Same procedure as every year, James.'"

The dialogue is from a comedy sketch filmed in Hamburg in glorious black-and-white in 1963. "Dinner for One, or the 90th Birthday" has become such a perennial staple on German television that at least one German airline even shows it on flights just before and after New Year's Day. Traditionally, Germans gather in front of their televisions every New Year's Eve (*Silvester*) to watch Miss Sophie and her butler, James, become increasingly tipsy.

Why is December 31 called *Silvester* in German? We don't know when Saint Sylvester—or Sankt Silvester—was born, but he was pope (*Papst*) from 314 until he died in Rome on December 31, 335. Legend says that Pope Sylvester cured Roman emperor Constantine I of leprosy (*Aussatz*)—after converting him to Christianity, of course. For this, the grateful emperor supposedly granted the pope the so-called Donation of Constantine, giving him extensive rights to land and power. (This gift now seems to be a forgery going back to the eighth century.)

However, New Year's Day has not always been January 1—even on the Christian calendar. In the early Middle Ages, most of Christian Europe celebrated the beginning of each new year on March 25 (Annunciation Day). The Anglo-Saxons started the new year on March 1 until William the Conqueror made January 1 New Year's Day. (England later returned to the March 25 date.) Although the Julian calendar of Rome had set January 1 as the start of the year, it was not until 1582, with the introduction of the Gregorian calendar, that most of Europe adopted the practice of beginning the year on the first day of January. Pope Gregory had the assistance of the German Jesuit mathematician Christopher Clavius (1537–1612) in refining his new calendar, but the Gregorian calendar was not adopted in German Protestant regions until 1700—and even later in many parts of the world, such as Britain (1751) and Russia (1918).

Einen Guten Rutsch!

Most German speakers are unaware that the traditional New Year's expression *einen guten Rutsch* has nothing to do with "sliding" (*rutschen*) into the New Year. It actually comes from the Hebrew word *rosh*, meaning "head" or "beginning"—thus, the beginning of a new year. Apparently, the expression came into German via the Yiddish expression for "a good beginning"—as in Rosh Hashanah, the Jewish New Year. That makes it just one of many German (and English) expressions that derive from Yiddish.

Related Web link: silvester-online.de—links to hotels and parties for New Year celebrations (G)

Credit/Debit Cards and Mobile Payment

In most of Europe, particularly in Britain, France, the Netherlands, and Scandinavia, you don't have to think twice about your credit card being accepted. In Germany, you do.

Beyond that, Germany and Austria have resisted the growing popularity of mobile payment, something so common in Sweden that cash has almost disappeared, even for small daily transactions. Only about 11 percent of Germans with a mobile phone made an in-store purchase using their phone in 2017; in the United States almost twice as many (20.5 percent) did so. While it is available in Switzerland, Apple Pay was not even an option in Germany in 2017. Android Pay and Samsung Pay are still just getting started. Germany's Sparkasse (savings bank) network did not introduce its mobile S-Payment product nationwide until mid-2018.

Germans prefer to pay with cash or a bank card. Unlike in neighboring France, Germans don't write checks, and their use of credit cards is far lower than in the United States and most of Europe. Berlin's public transport ticket machines did not accept credit card payment until late 2017 (but they accept only chip-and-PIN cards, not magnetic strip cards). Tourists usually will have no problem paying with plastic for a hotel stay, a rental car, a tank of gas, or a train ticket in Germany, but never assume that the nice restaurant in which you just dined will accept credit cards. Does that multilevel bookstore accept MasterCard or Visa for all those expensive maps and books you just selected? Better ask in advance, or get in the habit of carrying more cash on you in Germany than you would back home. And don't be fooled by the EC/Maestro debit card logo that looks a lot like the MasterCard one. (You have to have a German or EU bank account to get an EC debit card.) Stores that accept EC card payment may not always also take credit cards.

When do Germans use a credit card? When they're traveling outside Germany! Germans visiting the United States can use a credit card almost anywhere for almost anything, but an American in Germany can't do the same. Although credit card acceptance in Germany has improved over the years, it still hasn't reached U.S. levels, especially when you get off the tourist circuit and move into the local economy.

So what is behind this Teutonic aversion to credit cards? First, a German *Kreditkarte* is more like a debit card, requiring full payment of the balance at the end of each month. Plus, merchants don't like to pay the card transaction fees. But it may simply come down to this: The German word *Schuld* means both "debt" and "guilt."

Related Web links: eurocard.de—Eurocard Germany, MasterCard in Europe (G); visa.com—Visa International (E)

Shopping: A Brief History of *das Ladenschlussgesetz*

"We came, we saw, we did a little shopping." Contrary to that bit of graffito from the late Berlin Wall, Germany has never been especially kind to shoppers. Compared with most of the rest of Europe, the German-speaking countries have had a tradition of limited shopping hours and an attitude on the part of salespeople that turns the phrase "customer service" into an oxymoron. Non-Germans may find today's shopping hours in Germany a bit restrictive, but they should know how much more draconian the law was in the 1990s and before.

Germany's store closing law, *das Laden-schlussgesetz* dates back to 1956. Ostensibly to protect the German family and workers, the country's labor unions and shopkeepers long conspired to maintain hours that favored store owners and employees over customers. For decades, German stores could open their doors only from 7:00 A.M. until 6:30 P.M. on weekdays, and only from 7:00 A.M. until 2:00 P.M. on Saturdays (and once a month until 4:00 P.M., the so-called long Saturday). That was long after many German families had two breadwinners who found it very inconvenient to have stores closed when they got off work. An exception allowed bakeries to open a little earlier—Germans do like their fresh bread! In 1960, a small exception allowed stores to remain open until 6:30 P.M. on the four Advent Saturdays before Christmas. But on Sundays there was a virtual shopping blackout. Except for tourist areas, airports, train stations, restaurants, and gas stations (and their minimarts), "Never on Sunday" still takes on a whole new meaning in Germany.

Almost 30 years passed before the first small crack in the store-hours law appeared in 1989 with the introduction of the "long Thursday," on which stores could remain open until 8:30 P.M., although many smaller shops continued to close earlier.

Seven more years passed before a 1996 revision basically made every weekday a "long Thursday," but cut 30 minutes off the closing time. Retail businesses could now remain open from 6:00 A.M. to 8:00 P.M. Monday through Friday, and until 4:00 P.M. on Saturdays. In 2003, the law added four shopping hours to Saturday, meaning that stores could be open for business every day except Sunday and holidays from 6:00 A.M. to 8:00 P.M. Bakeries could open at 5:30 A.M. and, for the first time ever, four "shopping Sundays" (*verkaufsoffene Sonntage*) per year would be allowed (maximum 5 hours, closing by 6:00 P.M.).

Current shopping hours in Germany go back to June 2006, when Germany's 16 *Länder* (states) were allowed to make their own laws. See p. 29 for more.

Shopping Hours in Germany Today

Germany's store closing law, *das Laden-schlussgesetz*, first created in 1956, is called a store *closing* law, not a store *opening* law. In some *Länder* today, the law still states that shops and businesses must remain *closed* between the hours of 8:00 P.M. and 6:00 A.M., rather than *open* from 6:00 A.M. to 8:00 P.M. This reveals something about how German legislators think about shopping hours. Germany (and some of its German-speaking neighbors) has long had the most limited shopping hours in Europe (see p. 28).

The laws loosened gradually, but a huge change came in 2006. That was the year the Bundestag verified German federalism by allowing each of Germany's 16 *Länder* (states) to determine its own shopping hours. Federal law now applies only if a Land does not pass its own law. So far, only Bavaria has kept federal law. Berlin, on the other hand, was the first state to pass a much more liberal law for business hours, allowing up to 10 shopping Sundays per year and 24-hour opening times Monday through Saturday. (Note that just because stores *may* stay open does not mean they will!)

These new states' rights mean that shopping hours vary according to where you're located in Germany. In general, the further north you are, the longer the opening times are. Berlin, Brandenburg, Bremen, Hamburg, Hessen, Niedersachsen, and Schleswig-Holstein have all chosen to allow unrestricted hours, as has Baden-Württemberg, the only liberal outlier in the south. Although some allow "shopping Sundays," no state has chosen to allow unrestricted Sunday store hours.

According to a 2014 survey by the German polling firm GfK, 63 percent of Germans had taken advantage of special shopping Sundays (*verkaufsoffene Sonntage*), but only one in three would support eliminating the Sunday shopping ban entirely.

The Sunday shopping ban has contributed to the growth of the "*Späti*," short for *Spätverkaufsstelle* or *Spätkauf*, a type of hole-in-the-wall convenience store. (The term *Späti* was finally added to the *Duden*, Germany's semiofficial dictionary in 2017.) Berlin is best known for *Spätis* (an estimated 900!), but they are also found in Dresden, Leipzig, and a few other large cities. *Spätis* are open late and on Sundays, offering typical convenience store items. Despite some attempts to legalize them, they remain in a legal gray area. Like many things in Berlin, they are popular and the law looks the other way. On Sundays and late at night, most Germans have to settle for a grocery store in the local train station, or a gas station minimart.

Related Web links: berlin.de/special/shopping/adressen/spaetkauf—Spätifinder, Berlin (G); goethe.de/de/kul/mol/20422293.html—Spätis in Berlin (G)

Walmart's German Lesson

Walmart's spectacular failure in Germany—an estimated loss of at least one billion dollars—has become an iconic example of what not to do, and the topic of numerous academic papers and essays on adapting to a foreign business culture.

Despite its international success in a number of countries around the globe, Walmart stumbled badly in Germany. It had entered the German market, Europe's largest economy, in 1997 by acquiring 24 stores run by the German retail chain Wertkauf and another 74 stores belonging to Interspar. At the time of Walmart's acquisitions the two German retailers had only a 3 percent share of the German market. But Walmart had big plans to expand that share by introducing its "Every Day Low Prices" guarantee and a proven retail strategy that had worked so well in the United States, Mexico (starting in 1991), and the United Kingdom.

By the time Walmart was forced to abandon Germany in 2006, the giant American retailer realized it had ignored some key economic, legal, and cultural factors. What went wrong? How could Walmart succeed with over 100 stores in China, but fail so badly in Germany, a European culture closer to America's?

Where Walmart Went Wrong

- Walmart's imported retail practices (chanting employee warm-ups, plastic bags, smiling checkers, etc.) made Germans uncomfortable.
- Walmart management was unfamiliar with key German laws and regulations, including a strong union culture. Strict zoning requirements made it difficult for Walmart to find good new store locations. Other laws restricted opening hours and pricing in ways not present in other countries.
- Other German retailers were already using a low-price strategy when Walmart arrived. Walmart's prices were actually higher than those of some of its German competitors.
- German customers did not like some of Walmart's imported service practices, especially the smiling greeter who met them as they entered the store.
- Language barriers: Walmart had too many English-speaking managers who had trouble communicating with German-speaking employees and customers.

American companies such as Amazon, McDonald's, Starbucks, UPS, and others have learned how to achieve success in Germany, so Walmart being a U.S. American firm seems not to be a factor. Walmart failed to adequately research and prepare for the German market. It was a mistake similar to one Disney made in the early days of its amusement park outside Paris. Disney tried to impose on France its U.S. policy of serving no alcoholic beverages at Disney parks. *Sacre bleu!* That did not go over well in a culture of wine drinkers. However, unlike Walmart, once Disney noticed that European visitors were avoiding the park's restaurants because they couldn't order a glass of wine or beer, they changed that policy. Disney is still in France. Walmart is no longer in Germany.

Related Web links: edeka.de; rewe.de; lidl.de; aldi-nord.de; aldi-sued.de—Germany largest grocery chains

Die Post: Not Your Father's Post Office

Step into almost any German post office these days and you'll discover an entirely different place from what it was just a few years ago. Even before you enter *die Post*, the location itself speaks volumes about how radically this German institution has changed. The new modern black-and-yellow lighted Deutsche Post signs are seen increasingly in German shopping arcades. The traditional large central post office is giving way to many more conveniently located branches in places where Germans never saw a post office before.

Once you're inside, more indications of change become apparent. Instead of the former multitude of windows that were each designated for different postal services, Germany's privatized Deutsche Post AG now offers a multitude of services from any window. Customers can also order cellular telephone (*das Handy*) service, buy wrapping materials, and even pick up a greeting card to accompany the package. Rows of once hard-to-find post office boxes (*Postfach*) line the entryway. It's definitely not your father's post office anymore!

Although German post offices have always offered postal banking and telephone services, these are now presented in a more businesslike and attractive manner that reflects the splitting up of the former government-run Bundespost's three divisions: the mail (*die gelbe Post*, "yellow post"), telecommunications (now run by the separate Deutsche Telekom AG), and postal banking. Deutsche Post AG also owns the international express shipping company DHL.

Related Web link: **deutschepost.de**—German post office (G)

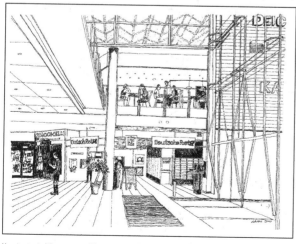

Here is a typical German post office in a modern shopping center.

31

E-Commerce in Germany

An early sign of the coming German online shopping revolution came in 1998, when the Regensburg-based online bookseller ABC Bücherdienst GmbH was bought by another e-commerce pioneer—Amazon. The American firm, founded only 3 years earlier by Jeff Bezos, soon expanded into selling far more than books in many countries all around the world. Today Amazon.de is the largest online retailer in Germany. Otto, which began as a mail-order catalog, is now Germany's number two online shopping site, followed by Zalando, Notebooksbilliger.de, Tchibo, and several others.

In 2016, a total of 74 percent of Germans made at least one purchase online in the previous 12 months, tied with the Dutch. (The United Kingdom led in Europe, with 83 percent, followed closely by Denmark's 82 percent.) Amazon's share of the online market in Germany has grown from a mere 11.2 percent in 2008 to a significant 38.5 percent in 2016. Based on the company's annual report, Amazon's total turnover for 2016 was estimated to be €12.78 billion ($14.15 billion USD) in Germany, which represents about 10 percent of Amazon's total worldwide sales. (Net sales increased 27 percent to $136.0 billion USD.)

According to the Centre for Retail Research, German consumers spent about 883 euros per capita for online purchases, making them second in the European Union. British online consumers ranked first, with an amount of 1,266 euros per person, while French online shoppers ranked third with per capita spending of about 745 euros.

The preferred payment method for Germans is different from most other Europeans. While most online shoppers prefer to use a credit or debit card for payment, only about 34 percent of Germans paid for an online purchase with a credit card. Almost 60 percent paid via direct bank draft (*Geldüberweisung*) at the time of purchase or later via an invoice. Other payment options were online services such as PayPal, GiroPay, ELV, or Sofort Überweisung. Online sales in Germany increased from a total of 37 billion euros in 2012 to 66.8 billion euros in 2016.

Global Websites Ranked by Language Percentage

Top 10 Languages used by the top 10 million websites, March 2017

English	51.6%
Russian	6.6%
Japanese	5.6%
German	5.6%
Spanish	5.1%
French	4.1%
Portuguese	2.6%
Italian	2.3%
Chinese	2.0%
Polish	1.7%

Source: W3Techs, estimated percentages

Language of Worldwide Internet Users—Percentage

Top 10 Internet User Languages, March 2017

English	25.2%
Chinese	20.4%
Spanish	7.9%
Arabic	4.6%
Indonesian	4.1%
Portuguese	4.1%
Japanese	3.2%
Russian	2.8%
French	2.7%
German	2.2%

Source: statista.com

Related Web links: ecommercenews.eu—e-commerce in the EU (E)

Questions You Should Ask—Part 1

Here are three questions you should ask yourself before leaving for Germany:

1. Will my credit or ATM cards work in Germany?

Most major credit cards (MasterCard, Visa, American Express) are accepted in shops and restaurants in Germany. Note, however, that credit cards are used less frequently in Germany than in North America and most other places. Some stores accept only German bank (EC) cards. Germans prefer cash and bank debit cards. It is wise to carry more cash than you might normally. ATMs (*Geldautomaten*) are widely available in Germany, so it is easy to get cash, but make sure you have a chip card with a PIN. Mobile phone payment (Android Pay, Apple Pay, etc.) is just beginning in Germany. (See "Credit/Debit Cards and Mobile Payment" for more.) Many credit cards charge a 3 percent "foreign transaction fee." If you use a card without that fee, you'll save money. Your bank may also charge an ATM fee.

2. Will my mobile phone (*das Handy*) work in Germany?

Europe has a single digital wireless standard (GSM) used by all mobile phone providers. In the United States, only AT&T and T-Mobile use the GSM mobile phone system. But most newer smartphones sold in North America are multiband/multisystem models that can also function in GSM countries. Most iPhones and Android phones will work in Europe, but you need to know what your provider charges for international roaming. Some are very reasonable, but others are not. Another solution for an unlocked phone is to buy a local SIM card that will work with your phone in Germany and Europe.

3. How about electricity and appliances?

German electricity comes in the 220-volt, 50-hertz (cycle) variety, which will destroy most North American 110-volt appliances without a voltage converter. Coming from most other non-Continental countries, you will also need a plug adapter for the German *Schukostecker* (safety plug) with their round prongs. Clocks, turntables, and other 60-hertz devices will not work properly in Germany because of the 10-cycles-per-second difference. For other large and small appliances, you can get transformers (*Transformatoren*) that will convert the voltage. North American television sets are not compatible with the German TV system.

Related Web links: americanexpress.com—American Express, select country (E, G); dinersclub.com—Diner's Club International (E); mastercard.de—MasterCard Germany (G); mastercard.us - MasterCard USA (E); visa.de—Visa Germany (G); visa.com—Visa USA (E)

Questions You Should Ask—Part 2

Here are four questions you should ask yourself in Germany:

1. Why are Germans so pushy? They don't seem to know what a line/queue is. This "pushy" behavior is not limited to Germans. It's a European thing. The European tendency for public aggression is also seen on the road. It means the meek will wait forever. When there's an opening, go for it. If you don't, a German will. This applies to getting on the bus or getting out of a traffic circle. You need to adjust to a different mentality that regards politeness as a sign of weakness, and regards smiling for no reason as a sign of a weak mind. One of the few locations where Germans will actually stand in line is at an ATM (*der Geldautomat*).

2. Why are Germans such fanatics when it comes to banning loud noise? This is a country with laws that prohibit mowing your lawn on Sunday or playing your piano after 8:00 p.m. . . . all in the cause of noise prevention. The reason is simple: excessive noise violates the sacred German right to privacy. A German's home is not only his or her castle—it's a private preserve. In a country with high population density and close living conditions, such laws are regarded as essential to civil order. Other signs of Germans' sacred privacy: closed doors, front-yard fences, and less use of first names.

3. Why should I take along my own shopping bag when I go out to buy groceries and many other items? Most German grocery stores and many other shops offer plastic or cloth bags, but for a price. They're usually not free. The majority of German shoppers automatically take their own *Einkaufstasche* to avoid paying extra for a store bag. To add insult to injury, you usually have to bag your own groceries! German checkers have it pretty soft; they also get to sit at the register while you're bagging the groceries they just rang up.

4. Do they serve beer at McDonald's in Germany? Yes, they do. (In France, they serve wine.) And that is just one of many differences between Germany and North America, only some of which involve alcohol. McDonald's Germany also serves coffee and soft drinks, but you usually have to ask for ice in your Coke or Sprite. The legal drinking age for alcohol (distilled spirits) in Germany is 18, but you only have to be 16 to legally drink beer or wine in public. If a parent or guardian is present, a 14-year-old may consume beer or wine in a restaurant or pub. Beer and wine can be purchased from vending machines, but only in places where underage people can't gain entry or if the vending machine is under constant supervision (as in a hotel).

Related Web link: mcdonalds.de—McDonald's Germany (G)

Rules for Dealing with Germans

Everyone is *not* alike!

1. Remember that Germans really hate rule breakers!

2. Germans and Americans do *not* think and act alike in social and business situations—especially in first encounters. Get over the myth that "we're all basically alike." It sounds good, but this mind-set is counterproductive.

3. Germans tend to be blunt, frank, and—to Anglo-American eyes—tactless in certain situations. They tend to correct you when you don't want to be corrected. That's because they are primarily concerned with exchanging facts and information, not "warm fuzziness." Since they also do this with other Germans, try to understand that you have not been singled out for special treatment.

4. Germans aren't into "idle chatter." They don't really care if you "have a nice day" (an expression they view as a symbol of American "superficiality"), and they don't want to talk about (a) their jobs, (b) their kids or family, or (c) the weather with a stranger (i.e., anyone they haven't known for at least a year or more). Such conversation is reserved for close friends.

5. Both the German language and the Germans draw a clear line between *Freunde* (*du/ihr*) and *Bekannte* (*Sie*), between private (home) and public (work). You are a *Bekannte(r)* ("acquaintance") and on *Sie* terms until your German counterpart says otherwise. This is one of the most difficult rules for easygoing, just-call-me-Bob Americans to truly grasp and internalize.

6. Germans have been known to smile, but unnecessary smiling is frowned on. A German needs a good reason to smile. In fact, excessive smiling for most Europeans is an indication of weak-mindedness. Don't overdo smiling around Germans. At heart, Germans are pessimists, and they enjoy their pessimism. Don't deprive them of that pleasure. Corollary to Rule 6: Never try to tell a joke in German. Leave this to professionals like Harald Schmidt (a well-known German night-show host) or Germans who have had too much to drink. Germans have a sense of humor, but it has no resemblance to either the American or British variety. It takes many years to delve into the German sense of humor.

7. Learn and accept Rules 1 through 6. Don't think you can (or should) change people. Learn to adjust to *them*, rather than expecting them to adjust to you. If you react with indignation or anger, even privately, then you are displaying a profound lack of understanding of the culture in which you're trying to function.

There are a few Germans who don't fit the preceding rules, but all six of them are now living in the United States or Canada.

Related Web link: german-way.com—Cultural and language info for expats and travelers in Germany (E)

35

In Case of Emergency in Germany: Dial 112 or 110

The universal emergency telephone number in Europe is 112. Similar to 911 in North America or 999 in the United Kingdom, dialing 112 will connect you with medical, police, or fire services. In Germany, there is also a separate emergency number (*Notrufnummer*) for the police (110), but if in doubt, you can call 112 and they will also contact the police if necessary.

In many EU nations you can also get emergency assistance in English. In some countries you may also be able to get a response to your emergency call in other foreign languages, including the language used in a neighboring country. The reality in Germany and in most other European countries is that emergency assistance in English may be available only in larger metropolitan areas. Just in case, it is wise to know some German phrases and vocabulary suitable for emergencies.

Austria and Switzerland also use 112. Like Germany, they have special emergency numbers for police, medical, poisoning, and other emergencies, but they are not the same as those in Germany. Those numbers are available online.

Poison Control (*Giftnotruf*)

In most parts of Germany, the emergency poison control number is (local prefix) + 19240. For example, in Berlin you would call (0)30 19240. In the eastern states of Mecklenburg-Vorpommern, Sachsen, Sachsen-Anhalt, and Thüringen, dial (0)361 730 730.

Contacting Your Consulate or Embassy

In some emergency cases you also may want to contact your home country's embassy or consulate for assistance. The telephone numbers below are for U.S. citizens who require emergency services such as assistance with the death, arrest, illness, abduction in process, or injury of an American citizen. This contact information is for the U.S. embassy in Berlin and the U.S. consular offices in Frankfurt am Main and Munich. Note: The U.S. Consulates in Düsseldorf, Hamburg, and Leipzig do not offer emergency services.

Berlin • U.S. Embassy
Pariser Platz 2
10117 Berlin
Tel. (030) 83050-0 (within Germany)
Tel. 01149 (30) 83050-0 (from the U.S.)
Web: de.usembassy.gov/u-s-citizen-services/emergency-contact/
Munich • U.S. Consulate General
Königinstraße 5
80539 München
Tel. (089) 2888-0 (within Germany)
Tel. 01149 (89) 2888-0 (from the U.S.)
Frankfurt am Main • U.S. Consulate General
Gießener Str. 30
60435 Frankfurt am Main
Tel. (069) 7535-0 (within Germany)
Tel. 01149 (69) 7535-0 (from the U.S.)

The following U.S. Consulates in Germany offer limited services only. For emergencies, contact the embassy or consulates listed above.

Düsseldorf—Serves residents of the state of North Rhine-Westphalia (NRW).
Willi-Becker-Allee 10, 40227 Düsseldorf
Hamburg—Serves residents of Hamburg, Bremen, Niedersachsen, Schleswig-Holstein, and Mecklenburg-Vorpommern.
Alsterufer 27/28, 20354 Hamburg
Leipzig—Serves residents of Saxony, Saxony-Anhalt, and Thuringia
Wilhelm-Seyfferth-Straße 4, 04107 Leipzig

Related Web links: de.usembassy.gov—U.S. Embassy & Consulates in Germany; **gov.uk/world/germany**—British help and services in Germany

Sie and *Du*: You and Thou Shouldn't Get Too Familiar

The rule for *you* in German is simple: When in doubt, use the formal *Sie*. Addressing a person as *du* when *Sie* would be correct is demeaning and expresses—whether you mean to or not—either an air of superiority or unwarranted familiarity on your part. Neither will help you win any German friends.

This little language detail is not as minor as English speakers may tend to think. Although the English form of *du—thou—* died out of English, it is alive and well in German and the other European languages. For some reason, the familiar *thou* of English faded away, while *du*, *tœ*, *tu*, and other familiar-*you* forms continue to be used in German, Spanish, French, and Italian. This distinction between the familiar *you* and the formal *you* serves a function that English speakers should not ignore. While *thou* is now seen only in poetry, the Bible, Shakespeare, and other sources of "olde English," its German equivalent serves an important role in modern German. The German equivalent of "ya'll" or "you guys" is *ihr*, the plural form of *du*.

To better understand this concept, relate it to similar situations in English. We may no longer have *thou*, but when talking to, for instance, Robert Johnson, we do address him as "Mr. Johnson" when "Bob" isn't appropriate—and this is more often the case in German than in English! Even though Americans may use first names before they know someone's last name, the fact is that under certain conditions, addressing someone as "Mr." or "Mrs." is the right thing to do. Germans use *Sie*—the formal *you*—to accomplish this social acknowledgment.

White-collar workers generally use *Sie*. In fact, Germans who have worked together in the same office for many years will often continue to address each other as *Sie*.

Blue-collar workers, on the other hand, use *du*. This familiar form of *you* is also used by members of certain other social groups, such as students and soldiers. Likewise, the familiar *du* is common among family members; between good friends; and for children, God, and pets. Although there has been a tendency among the younger generation to use *du* sooner and more often than their elders, this is not always the case. To avoid those unfortunate miscues, it is wise to wait for your German friends (*Freunde*) and acquaintances (*Bekannte*) to initiate the use of *du*—remembering that Germans make a clear distinction between *Freunde* and *Bekannte*.

"Fräulein" or "Frau"? "Du" or "Sie"?

Only in Germany would you find a 2,000-word newspaper essay on the dilemma of how to address a waitress in a restaurant. A recent article in the *Frankfurter Rundschau* reflects an aspect of German culture that is sometimes difficult for Germans, much less *Ausländer*, to understand: the various levels of formality or informality (mixed in with political correctness) reflected in the German language.

At some point in the early 1970s as the *Frauenbewegung* (women's movement) was taking hold, it became a faux pas to try to get your waitress's attention by shouting out, "*Fräulein!*" (FROY-line, "Miss!"). Any woman above the age of about 18, married or not, could no longer be addressed as "Miss." Rather than adopt a new word like the English term *Ms.*, German logically proclaimed that henceforth, just as *Herr* (Mr.) applied to any adult male, the existing title *Frau* (Mrs.) would apply to any adult woman, including waitresses. This elegantly avoided the "Ms." problem that still plagues English. Soon, however, Germans realized that they had created a new problem. While it had been socially acceptable to shout "*Fräulein*" across a room filled with diners, no respectable German woman was going to put up with being addressed as simply "*Frau*" without her last name. It just sounds so wrong in German!

So, now Germans are still faced with the addressing-the-waitress dilemma. Neither the German Hotel and Restaurant Association (DEHOGA) nor the Association of Hotel and Service Personnel has been able to suggest a good alternative. Some restaurants have adopted the once radical idea of putting American-style name tags on their waitresses. (This in a culture that sees no problem in two people who have worked together in an office for 15 years still calling each other "Mr. So-and-so" or "Mrs. So-and-so" rather than using their first names.) The name tags allow patrons to call a waitress by her last name: "*Frau Schmidt!*" Some restaurants have even been using first-name tags, a most un-German thing to do!

Fashion in Germany

Germany may not be the first country you think of when you hear "fashion designers," but think again. German designers such as Jil Sander, Karl Lagerfeld, Hugo Boss, and Wolfgang Joop have been around long enough for most people to know their names. But some more recent German fashion designers may not be as familiar: Annelie Augustin (since 2009), Bobby Kolade (launched his own label in 2013), Leyla Piedayesh (her lala Berlin brand has been a hit), and Karlotta Wilde (won the Premium Young Designers Award in 2011). The multitalented German-American model Heidi Klum turned fashion designer when she debuted her clothing line for Jordache in 2008, following the earlier success of her Mouawad jewelry collection. In 2017, Klum released the fashion line Heidi & the City for exclusive sale in Lidl grocery stores.

Although the German fashion industry is still spread among many German towns and cities, the undisputed center of the German fashion world is now Berlin, a position it assumed only recently. For years, Cologne, Düsseldorf, and Munich were Germany's dominant fashion centers. That began to change in 2003, when Karl-Heinz Müller first moved his Bread & Butter denim-and-streetwear exhibition from Cologne to the capital. After some false starts and a few delays in Berlin, the first Mercedes Benz Fashion Week in the summer of 2007 drew more attention to the German capital city. Berlin moved closer to becoming Germany's fashion capital in July 2009, when the Bread & Butter returned from Barcelona, where it had established itself as a major event after leaving Berlin.

Now the Bread & Butter is a leading trade fair for urban fashion and ready-to-wear trends, held during the Berlin Fashion Week (*Berliner Modewoche*) twice annually, in January and July. Other Fashion Week events include the Premium Exhibitions, the Bright Tradeshow, Show&Order, Panorama, and the Selvedge Run. Almost half a dozen fashion shows also take place. Berlin's Fashion Week, now held in front of the Brandenburg Gate, has grown in importance every year since its debut.

Aspiring fashion designers in Germany can choose from some 40 respected schools of design, including the Weißensee Kunsthochschule/Art Academy in Berlin, and the Akademie Mode & Design in Düsseldorf.

Yet Berliners and most Germans are not really known for being very fashion-conscious. Unless they work in a bank or in upper management, few Germans, male or female, ever wear a suit to work. Most German men consider "dressed up" to be a sports coat with jeans and no tie. Women generally prefer plain Birkenstocks over fancy high heels. It may take a while before Berlin is more like Paris or Milan.

Related Web Links: vogue.de—see *Society, Who Is Who*, for information on Wolfgang Joop, Karl Lagerfeld, Jil Sander, and Claudia Schiffer (G); **hugoboss.com/de**—Hugo Boss corporate website (E, G); **lederhosenmuseum.de**—Virtual Lederhosen Museum (E, G); **deutscheshaus.cc** for German products (E)

Das Bad or *das WC*? Germans Don't "Go to the Bathroom"!

There are three essential facts to know about this delicate subject: (1) the German terms for *men/gentlemen* and *ladies*, (2) the difference between a bathroom and a toilet, and (3) how to ask where the "rest room" is.

First of all, the German language is more direct and uses far fewer euphemisms than English when it comes to basic bodily functions in general and to the place for "relieving oneself" in particular. In German, you call a toilet a toilet (*eine Toilette, das WC*). It's not a "rest" room, a "powder" room, the "loo," or the "john"—it's the room with a toilet, *die Toilette*. The closest German comes to toilet euphemisms are words borrowed from English: *das WC*, short for "water closet" and pronounced VAY-SAY, or the somewhat less refined *das Klo*. On the autobahn and in some public places, you'll also see the symbol "00" (*null, null*). Generally, but not always, "00" means an outhouse-style, hole-in-the-ground, water-less type of toilet, whereas "WC" always denotes a flush toilet.

The toilet is certainly never the bathroom! If you go to the "bathroom" in Germany, it is to take a bath. Although *das amerikanische Badezimmer* has gained favor over the years in German homes, hotels, and other places, the traditional German approach has long been to separate the two activities by locating them in different rooms. The "bath" or "bathing" room is called, logically, *das Badezimmer* or *das Bad*. It contains a bathtub (*die Badewanne*) and/or a shower (*die Dusche*) but usually no toilet. The toilet or water closet may be located in its own room next door or even farther down the hall. So, if you inquire of your German host, "*Wo ist das Badezimmer?*" you are likely to get a somewhat startled look that asks, "You want to take a bath now?" If you want to use the facilities, just ask: "*Wo ist die Toilette, bitte?*" In public places, the ladies' room is marked "*Damen*" or "D," the men's room "*Herren*" or "H." Most German public toilets have an attendant, who expects a tip to be left in the dish strategically placed near the exit. Also, it is wise, to carry some change for pay toilets, which are common in Germany.

"*Wo der Kaiser auch zu Fuss geht*" is one of the few euphemistic toilet expressions in German. It refers to "where even the emperor has to walk" and is used in a humorous way rather than to avoid the actual word *toilet*. A shorter version is simply "*Ich muss wohin*" ("I must go there [where the emperor . . .]"). Other ways to say you've gotta go: *Ich muss . . . aufs Klo/auf die Toilette/aufs WC*.

This is a typical German hotel bathroom, complete with toilet and bidet.

Weights and Measures: Give 'em an Inch and They'll Take a Meter

When the $125 million Mars Climate Orbiter apparently burned up in the Martian atmosphere in September 1999, it was a spectacular example of how confusion over different systems of weights and measures can lead to problems. The orbiter met its fiery fate only because the scientists had mistakenly fed it data calculated in British pounds instead of the metric newtons (units of force) that the spacecraft's computer was expecting.

The Anglo-American system of weights and measures makes its last stand in the United States and, to a lesser degree, in Great Britain. The English system itself varies from country to country in the former British Empire, often in mysterious ways. For purposes of conversion, the following table compares the U.S. version of the Anglo-American system, since the United States is about the only place the older system is still being used in everyday life.

Germany and the rest of Europe use the metric system that was first proposed in France in 1791 before gradually being accepted throughout the civilized world—that is, everywhere but in the former American colonies. Even there, both the U.S. yard and pound were legally defined in metric terms after 1893. In Europe, too, there are a few measurement oddities. For instance, TV screen measurements and tire sizes for cars and bikes are expressed in inches (*Zoll*), not centimeters. Also, horsepower (*Pferdestärke*), rather than the official watts or joules, continues to be used commonly in Germany and elsewhere.

These international measurement differences become more than abstract math problems when an American starts looking for a 150-square-meter apartment in Germany (150 *Quadratmeter* 3 10.7641 square feet 5 1,614.615 square feet). On the road, it is relatively simple to convert kilometers to miles or vice versa, but it can be a nightmare trying to convert miles per gallon to *Liter auf 100 Kilometer*. That's why we offer the following conversion charts.

Temperature

FAHRENHEIT	CELSIUS
230	110
212	100
(boiling point of water)	
194	90
176	80
158	70
140	60
122	50
104	40
98.4	37
(normal body temperature)	
86	30
70	21
(room temperature)	
68	20
50	10
32	0
(freezing point of water)	
14	−10
−4	−20
−22	−30
−40	−40

Miles per Gallon (MPG)/*Liter auf 100 Kilometer* (L/100 KM)

MPG	L/100 KM	L/100 KM	MPG
20	11.761	10	23.5
25	9.409	9	26.13
30	6.72	8	29.40
35	6.72	7	33.60
40	5.88	6	39.20

Related Web links: metric-conversions.org—metric conversions (E)

This depicts Wednesday, August 2 at 2:38 P.M. on a German clock and calendar.

16 *Länder*, 16 School Systems

The German educational system follows the European model of free public education and a variety of secondary schools for academic and vocational education, rather than the American model of a single comprehensive high school for all students. However, as in the United States, educational matters in Germany are primarily the responsibility of each of the 16 states, or *Länder*. The 16 state systems are coordinated to some extent by the federal German Ständige Konferenz der Kultusminister (Standing Conference of Education Ministers) and a 1971 agreement (Hamburger Abkommen) among the *Länder* that created a higher degree of uniformity in a system that at one time had students starting the school year in the spring in some states, and in the fall in others.

With reunification in 1990, Germany had to solve the problem of integrating the former Communist East German school system of the five "New States" into the existing system of the Federal Republic. Students in the eastern German states, for instance, still graduate after 12 years of schooling, versus 13 years in most of the western states. Also, most schools in the East still have a lunch cafeteria, while most in the West do not.

Germany requires 12 years of schooling, from age 6 to 18. Just how and in which kind of school those years are spent depends on whether a student chooses an academic or a vocational (*Berufschule*) track. In any case, the German constitution (*Grundgesetz*) makes religious instruction a compulsory subject in German schools, though parents and students may opt out when the student reaches a certain age.

Since kindergarten (children's garden) is a German invention, it may be surprising to learn that kindergarten is usually not a part of the German public school system, and attendance is voluntary. Most German kindergartens are run by churches or other nonprofit organizations. Some are even company sponsored. In the East, however, the so-called *Kinderkrippen* preschools are still part of the school system. Although kindergarten has traditionally been popular, and more than 65 percent of kindergarten-age children enroll, it wasn't until 1996 that all German parents attained the legal right to have their children attend kindergarten.

At age six, all German children go to *Grundschule*, usually grades one through four. After that, there are many secondary school choices: *Hauptschule* (five to six years of general education), *Realschule* (six-year academic curriculum), *Gesamtschule* (comprehensive curriculum), or *Gymnasium* (nine-year academic curriculum). Students who wish to attend a university must graduate with an *Abitur* school-leaving certificate, usually from a *Gymnasium*. One educational option is definitely not available in Germany: Home schooling. German law requires school attendance. Several lawsuits have resulted in German court decisions confirming the illegality home schooling.

Related Web link: schulweb.de——German schools online (G); bildungsserver.de——Deutscher Bildungsserver (G); eduserver.de——Education in Germany (E)

School Choice: *Wer die Wahl Hat, Hat die Qual.* (He Who Has a Choice Has Torture.)

When Americans debate the issue of school choice, they may want to take a look at the German education system. It is a system of many choices, including not only *which* school to attend but also which *kind* of school to attend. While the German school system has some problems of its own, one of them is not lack of choice.

German students and their parents have an almost bewildering array of options when it comes to education. In fact, one criticism of the German "multischool" system is that it forces students and parents to make such important choices too early. In most *Länder* (education is a state matter, not a federal matter, in Germany), students must pass exams and decide after their fourth school year, at the tender age of 10, whether they will attend a *Hauptschule*, a *Realschule*, a *Gesamtschule*, or a *Gymnasium*. (There are *Sonderschulen* for special education.) Each of the secondary-school categories has a different course of study and a different educational goal. (See the table.) Although alternatives are possible—including the so-called orientation phase in grades five and six, which allows students to switch schools in the seventh grade, and the *zweiter Bildungsweg* (second educational path) of evening remedial schools—the German system is fairly rigid once a path has been chosen.

Partly in response to this inflexibility, some states introduced the *Gesamtschule*, or comprehensive high school, in the 1960s. But the *Gesamtschule*, which combines the three traditional school types under one roof, has met with limited success in only a few *Länder*. It has been associated with a lowering of standards, particularly for earning an *Abitur*, the vital German secondary school diploma required for university study. While in the 1970s, only about 11 percent of students graduated with an *Abitur* and went on to a university, in the 1990s, that figure had climbed to 34 percent.

Whichever kind of school the student chooses to attend, he or she can opt for almost any school in the community. German schools compete with each other for students, and Germany's outstanding public transportation system makes it possible for students to attend a school on the other side of town from where they live. Of course, a student may or may not be accepted by a school and may have to choose an alternative.

Type of School	Age Range	Certification Awarded
Hauptschule	10–15	*Hauptschulabschluss*
Realschule	10–16	*Realschulabschluss*
Gymnasium	10–19	*Abitur*
Berufsaufbauschule (integrated)	16–17	*Fachhochschulreife*
Fachoberschule (specialized)	16–18	*Fachhochschulreife*
Fachschule (technical)	16–18	*Fachhochschulreife*
Berufsfachschule (vocational)	16–18	*Fachhochschulreife*

Kita, Kindergarten, and Childcare

Kindergarten is a German invention that has spread around the world, but what is this institution like in its homeland? How does it fit into the German education system and daycare for children? To understand that, we also have to discuss the *Kindertagesstätte* (KiTa/Kita; "children's day place/home") and its variations. For purposes of discussion, we'll use the general, inclusive term that most people use: "Kita" (KEE-tuh).

Since education and childcare matters are regulated by the 16 states in Germany, there are differences, but in general, all across Germany there are three main types of Kita institutions that offer education and daytime supervision for young children: *die Kinderkrippe* (ages 6 months to 3 years), *der Kindergarten* (ages 2½ to 6), and *der Hort* or *Schulhort* (after-school or vacation care for elementary or secondary pupils). Austria and Switzerland have something similar, but unlike in Germany, kindergarten in Switzerland is part of the public school system.

Kitas in Germany may be run by a church, a nonprofit organization, a private company (often state-subsidized), or the local or state government. Although public funding comes from the federal and state governments, the quality and availability of Kitas varies drastically from state to state. Costs rose when in 2007 German lawmakers decided to expand Kitas to cover children under 3 years of age. Berlin and some eastern states offer Kita for children as young as 1 year, but it can be difficult to obtain a spot. Federal law mandates the right to a half-day in a nearby Kita for all children from age 4 until they enter first grade, a goal that has yet to be fully achieved everywhere in Germany. In 2016, Baden-Württemberg was the only state that had met the national standards.

Kitas are considered primarily a social service for families. While they do offer some pedagogical elements, the emphasis is on providing a safe, comfortable place for children while their parents are working. Only about 5 percent of Kita teachers and staff are male. The goal is to get that figure closer to 20 percent in the near future. Both training and pay will have to improve before that can happen.

The cost to place a child in a Kita varies according to many factors, including place of residence (city, state, region), services offered, hours per week, and the income level of the parent(s). Where Kita openings are limited, preference is given to single parents. Typical monthly costs range from 400 to 850 euros, depending on the factors mentioned above. Some states (Berlin, Hamburg) offer Kita vouchers to low-income families. Kita expenses are also tax-deductible. Rheinland-Pfalz is the only state in which Kita is free from the age of 2.

Related Web link: german-way.com—for information on preschool and daycare enrollment (E)

Higher Education and German Universities

In 1809, Wilhelm von Humboldt founded the *Universität zu Berlin*, later named for him and his brother Alexander. The "Humboldt-ian" university became a model for Europe. The German system of higher education is very different from the Anglo-American system. One of the biggest contrasts is that German university students pay no tuition fees. Their only costs are for books, minor administrative fees, and room and board. But some critics point out that you get what you pay for.

Over the years there has been criticism of Germany's *Hochschulen* (colleges and universities) from students, faculty, politicians, and others. The infamous 1968 student riots and the protests in 1997 were a result of German students often facing overcrowded lecture halls, limited major choices, uninspired teaching, and other deficiencies.

Recent attempts to reduce such failings with additional funding through tuition fees ended in failure. Students accustomed to zero tuition were not happy about even modest tuition charges of 500 euros per semester. After seven German states introduced university tuition fees (*Studiengebühren*) between 2004 and 2007, there was strong resistance. By 2014, the only two German states still charging tuition, Bavaria (*Bayern*) and Lower Saxony (*Niedersachsen*) had thrown in the towel.

Most states still charge a so-called *Semesterbeitrag* (semester fee) that ranges from 50 to 300 euros. American students consider that an extreme bargain, and they and other non-German students can take advantage of zero tuition fees. Some German universities now offer instruction in English for certain fields. Nevertheless, some knowledge of German is a necessity if you plan to attend a university in Germany.

Although the number of private academies, colleges, and universities (*Unis*) in Germany has increased over recent decades, for historical reasons they make up only about 100 of Germany's total of 850 institutions of higher learning. Critics cite this low number as an example of how little competition there is for the public universities. The German aversion to elitism means that public *Unis* are supposed to be "equals." In many cases this means they are mediocre, more provincial, and less cosmopolitan.

Recent efforts to introduce more competition with private, more international universities have had some success. Jacobs University Bremen is a private, English-language university that opened in 2001 (as the International University Bremen). In 2017, Jacobs had 1,399 students from 110 countries, including exchange students. Tuition ranges from 10,000 to 30,000 euros per academic year, depending on the course of study.

At Witten/Herdecke University, a private institution in the Ruhr, German is, exclusively, the language of instruction for the faculties of Health and of Arts and Humanities. The Faculty of Management and Economics offers three bilingual (English/German) degree programs. The international master's degree program is taught exclusively in English. Tuition options include pay-after-graduation, income-based payment, and other options.

Related Web links: **jacobs-university.de**—Jacobs University Bremen (E); **uni-wh.de**—Witten/Herdecke University (G), **uni-wh.de/en** (E); **ranking.zeit.de/che/de**—German university CHE rankings (G); **daad.org**—German Academic Exchange Service €

From German-Language Book to Hollywood Screenplay

Few moviegoers are aware of it, but Hollywood has a long record of drawing on German, Austrian, and Swiss sources for its movies, past and present. *The Sorcerer's Apprentice* (2010), starring Nicolas Cage, is only one of several films based on a traditional German story that was popularized in verse form by Johann Wolfgang von Goethe (see p. 10) as "Der Zauberlehrling" in 1797. The "Sorcerer's Apprentice" segment in Disney's animated film *Fantasia* (1940) is another example, reappearing in *Fantasia 2000*.

From Walt Disney to Miramax, from *Bambi* to *The Parent Trap*, Hollywood has often gone to the Germanic well for movie material. While the films may be famous, the original Austrian and German authors generally are not. Besides obvious borrowing, such as *The Sound of Music* (1965), based on the true-life story of the Austrian von Trapp family, many familiar Hollywood productions are derived from unfamiliar sources.

The Austrian writer Felix Salzmann (1869–1945), who wrote under the name Felix Salten, was the author of *Bambi: A Life in the Woods* (1923), *Bambi's Children*, and other animal tales. Few fans of Disney's 1942 animated classic *Bambi* have ever heard of Salten. Disney used another Salten work, "The Hound of Florence" (*Der Hund von Florenz*, 1923), as the basis for *The Shaggy Dog* (1959). The film, starring Fred MacMurray and Tommy Kirk, is about a boy who is changed into a dog. The studio never really publicized Salten's contribution to either film. Salten was living in Switzerland at the time of his death, only 3 years after *Bambi*'s release.

Disney was not much more forthcoming when the studio released *The Parent Trap* in 1961, with Hayley Mills in the dual role of twin sisters separated by the divorce of their parents. The film was based on a book by the German author Erich Kästner, *Das doppelte Lottchen*. In Kästner's novel, Luise and Lotte (played by real twin sisters in a 1950 German film) pull their identity switch in Munich and Vienna. The 1998 Hollywood remake (with Lindsay Lohan as Annie and Hallie) stays true to the tale-of-two-countries idea, transforming Germany and Austria into the United States and the United Kingdom.

Stanley Kubrick's *Eyes Wide Shut* (1999) was based on Arthur Schnitzler's erotic novella *Traumnovelle*, a 1920s Austrian work set in fin de siècle Vienna. Kubrick's screenplay transported the characters to 20th-century New York. Kubrick is just one of many filmmakers who have borrowed, adapted, and even stolen material originally written in German.

NOTE: If you'd like to view the original films (or books), Amazon and Netflix are good sources of German and other foreign-language movies.

Going to the Movies—*Wir gehen ins Kino*

With the global spread of multiscreen cineplexes, and Hollywood's world domination of cinematic entertainment, going to the movies (*ins Kino gehen*) in the Western world is pretty much the same experience anywhere—except for the language.

In Germany and Austria, non-German movies are almost always dubbed into German (*synchronisiert*). The Swiss, with a smaller market and three major languages, tend to use subtitles, *Untertitel*. Despite a vibrant German film and TV industry, about 70 to 85 percent of the motion pictures that Germans watch in a given year still come from Hollywood and other non-German studios, and dubbing is a big business. German film and voice actors stand in for Hollywood stars. Only very famous English-speaking actors usually have the same German voice all the time. Hearing a different German voice in different films can be disconcerting for people who are used to hearing the actors' real voices.

However, larger German cities such as Berlin, Cologne, Frankfurt, Hamburg, Munich, and Stuttgart have cinemas that regularly show English-language movies with the original soundtrack, usually without subtitles. German newspapers and websites indicate such films with "OF" or "OV" (original version), "O-Ton" (original sound), or "OmU" (original with German subtitles). Note that these designations also apply to films originally in French, Spanish, or other languages, not just English.

As in most places, German movie theaters sell snacks, but you may get a surprise with your popcorn. Germans prefer sugar on their popcorn rather than salt, but most theaters sell both. Also it's not unusual to have beer and wine in addition to soft drinks.

Germany has two main film production centers, with studios in Munich (Geiselgasteig, Bavaria Film Studio) and Potsdam (Studio Babelsberg), where domestic and Hollywood productions are made, including blockbusters like *The Hunger Games: Mockingjay Part 2* (2015, *Die Tribute von Panem—Mockingjay Teil 2*) and *The Grand Budapest Hotel* (2014). Most Hollywood films are released later in Germany/Europe than in the United States, but that is not always the case.

Blu-ray, DVD, and video streaming services such as Netflix Germany and Amazon.de offer the option of viewing English-language productions in German or English. German and European DVD, Blu-ray, and 4K/UHD discs are usually released with soundtracks in several languages, with or without subtitles. Note: European videos are not always compatible with North American players or devices.

Related Web links: cinemaxx.de—*Cinemaxx*, a large German movie theater chain, at whose site you can find films now showing in cinemas all over Germany (G); **kino.de**—movie news, background stories, and film listings (G); **kino-berlin.de**—find any movie now playing in Berlin, including OmU and OV movies in English (G); **kinonews.de**—a film and entertainment news site with an online movie-ticket service (G); **cinema.de**—Cinema Online, the Web version of Germany's largest movie magazine (G); cinestar.de—major German cinema chain; **imdb.com/calendar/?region=de**—upcoming releases in Germany (E)

ENTERTAINMENT

In the 1950s and '60s, movie stars such as Romy Schneider and Sophia Loren celebrated their first big successes at what was considered Germany's most glamorous cinema. The Zoo Palast was renovated and reopened in 2013.

Popular Music *auf Deutsch*: The German Music Scene

The modern German sound of music is rarely heard outside German-speaking Europe. There have been some notable exceptions over the years: "Autobahn" by Kraftwerk (1974), "Major Tom (völlig losgelöst/Coming Home)" by Peter Schilling (1982/83), "Der Kommissar" (1982) and "Rock Me Amadeus" (1985) by Austria's Falco, "99 Luftballons" by Nena (1989), "Du hast" by Rammstein (1997), and "Übers Ende der Welt" (2007) by Tokio Hotel. But for the most part, German rock, punk, and hip-hop artists are inaudible and invisible beyond the German-speaking world.

Thanks to Germany's home market of 82 million (plus another 13 million in Austria and Switzerland), German-language musical artists can survive and even prosper performing exclusively *auf Deutsch*. But anyone listening to music on the radio in Germany might think they're in Britain or the United States rather than Germany. The majority of the songs played on the air, 85 to 90 percent, have English or even Spanish lyrics, despite the fact that in recent years 8 of 10 albums on the official German sales charts were in German.

Even without a French-style law setting a quota for German-language music on the air, most German artists record and perform their songs exclusively or mostly in German. Non-Germans may never have heard of Die Ärzte, Die toten Hosen (punk); Die Prinzen, Silbermond, Wir sind Helden (rock); Herbert Grönemeyer, Ich + Ich (pop); Die fantastischen Vier (hip hop); Helene Fischer (folk); Xavier Naidoo (R&B); 2raumwohnung (electro-pop); and many other German artists/groups that sing in German and are mostly unknown in the English-speaking world.

That doesn't mean there aren't German bands that perform in English. You may not even realize that some big international hits were by German artists. The Scorpions had several successes in English, including "Wind of Change" in 1990, which became an anthem for the fall of the Wall, and "Rock You Like a Hurricane" (1984). Remember 1999's catchy "Mambo No. 5"? That was sung by Munich-born David Lubega, aka Lou Bega. Another Bavarian, Harold Faltermeyer, went to Hollywood and had a blockbuster hit with the "Axel F" theme he wrote for *Beverly Hills Cop* (1984). Faltermeyer later created music for *Top Gun* (1986) and other major movies.

Max Raabe and his Palast Orchester are an interesting example of international success, featuring songs from the 1920s and 1930s plus old-style original tunes. Singing in German and sometimes in English, Raabe regularly tours in Europe and North America. Most of his concerts sell out.

Related Web links: falco.at—although Falco is no longer with us, his website is (E); **fanta4.de**—fan page of German group Fanta4 (G); **groenemeyer.de**—Herbert Grönemeyer, more than a dozen CD albums (G); **kraftwerk.com**—their techno sounds started in the 1970s (G); **nena.de**—99 red balloons and all that (G); **dieprinzen.de**—Die Prinzen, a group from eastern Germany (G); **rammstein.de**—not for everyone, but their heavy-metal sounds (in German) are also popular outside of Germany (G); **udo-lindenberg.de**—Udo Lindenberg (G); **laut.de**—a German music site (G); **palast-orchester.de**—Max Raabe and his Palast Orchester (G, E)

Der Wein: A Brief German Wine Guide

German wines in general are the Rodney Dangerfield of the wine world. They tend not to get the respect reserved for French or even better California wines. The reasons are complex but in part have been self-inflicted. In the 1960s and 1970s, German vintners created a bad image for themselves when they exported crate upon crate of sugary sweet wines known as Blue Nun, Schwarze Katz, and Liebfraumilch, which long overshadowed the finer wines that Germany produces. Germany further shot itself in the foot by refusing to allow its wine makers to indicate on their labels the growing location (*Lage*) of the grapes used for a particular vintage's production. Labels may indicate the district, or *Anbaugebiet*, but that is a more general distinction than the *Lage*. Under German wine law, the label also provides a great deal of information about the grape harvest (six categories from early to late) and the sugar content (the Öchsle scale of sweetness or dryness). Unfortunately, none of these label criteria has anything to do with the quality of the wine—but they will tell you in detail just how sweet (*süß*) or dry (*trocken*) a given wine is.

Today, however, serious wine connoisseurs know that Germany (like Austria) produces some of the world's finest wines, white wines in particular. (Only approximately 10 percent of German production is red wine.) Germany's 13 wine regions from Ahr to Württemberg (and Austrian areas such as the Wachau, Neusiedlersee, and South Styria) produce many different wines of top quality. German wine by law is either *Tafelwein* (common table wine) or *Qualitätswein* (quality wine). This latter category is further divided into two sub-categories: *Qualitätswein bestimmter Anbaugebiete* (QbA), which is quality wine from a designated region, and *Qualitätswein mit Prädikat* (QmP), quality wine with special attributes, the highest category. A QmP wine may contain no added sugar, while a QbA wine is permitted to compensate for Germany's short, cool growing season with additional sugar. The label of a *Qualitätswein mit Prädikat* carries one of six *Prädikate* (attributes) that indicates the grape's degree of ripeness (and thus, sweetness) at harvest: *Kabinett* (first harvest, the driest), *Spätlese, Auslese, Beerenauslese, Eiswein*, and *Trockenbeerauslese* (the sweetest, from grapes dried on the vine). Most German wine is produced from the Riesling, Sylvaner, Müller-Thurgau, and Gewürztraminer grape varieties.

> **Prost!**
> The German equivalent of "Cheers" is *"Prost!"*

Brot und Wurst

*In der Not ißt man die Wurst auch ohne
Brot!*

(SPRICHWORT)

*In an emergency one even eats sausage
without bread!*

(PROVERB)

The two vital staples of the German diet are
bread (*Brot*) and sausage (*Wurst*). Often
served up together to create *ein heißes
Würstchen*, the Germanic equivalent of a
hot dog, these are the two dietary ingredients most associated with German cooking,
deutsche Küche. Only the beverage known
as "liquid bread"—beer (*Bier*)—can even
come close in importance; sauerkraut is a
distant fourth. Despite the more recent
invasion of American fast food, Italian pizza,
Turkish *Döner Kebap*, and other "foreign"
comestibles, the Germanic version of
McDonald's has long been the *Würstelbude,
Würstchenstand*, or *Wurstmaxe* (sausage
stand). A *Currywurst* (diced bratwurst with

ketchup and curry powder) could be called
the German national favorite.

The fact that there are more than 200
kinds of bread and 1,500 sausage varieties
illustrates the importance of these elements
in the diet of people in the German-speaking
world. Bread, in many shapes and colors, is
ever present in shops and restaurants and
on dining tables. The *Bäckerei* ("bakery")
has always been the one big exception to
Germany's strict laws concerning opening
hours (*Ladenschluss*), with bakeries allowed
to open much earlier than regular shops
and stores in order to provide the Germans,
Austrians, and Swiss with their fresh daily
bread. They buy their *Brot* in the form of
rolls (*Brötchen, Semmeln*) or in a wide variety of loaves known by so many names that
it would be impossible to list most of them
here. A few of the more common terms are
Weißbrot (white bread), *Schwarzbrot* (dark
bread), *Bauernbrot* (coarse rye bread),
Roggenbrot (rye bread), and *Salzstangel*
(salted rolls).

Wurst Expressions and Sayings

Alles hat ein Ende, nur die Wurst hat zwei.	Everything has an end; only the sausage has two.
Das ist mir Wurst.	It's all the same to me.
Es geht um die Wurst.	It's time to fish or cut bait.
kleines Würstchen	small-time operator, small-fry
Wurstblatt	a rag (in reference to a newspaper)
Wurstmaxe	sausage stand, vendor (derives from a Berlin vendor who called himself "*Akademischer Wurstmaxe*")
wurstig	indifferent, trifling, unimportant
Wurst wider Wurst	tit for tat

FOOD AND DRINK

Related Web links: brot.de—Deutsches Brot provides photos of 25 kinds of German bread (G); landlopers.com/2014/06/01/currywurst—description of the popular dish known as Currywurst (E)

This German *Metzgerei* offers a multitude of sausage types.

Das Bier: From Bock to Lager

Both the German and the English words for the ancient beverage known as beer—the alcoholic refreshment made from barley and sometimes wheat and other grains—may be derived from the Anglo-Saxon word for barley, *baere*. That evolved into Old English *bere* and Old High German *bior*—and eventually into *beer* and *Bier*.

No one knows when or where the first beer or beerlike beverage was brewed, but it is likely that prehistoric cultures drank an alcoholic beverage made from fermented grains. Beer was an important drink in ancient cultures as diverse as the Egyptians, the Incas, the Sumerians, and the Chinese. In what is now Germany, the Germanic tribes were brewing a meadlike beer at least eight hundred years before the Romans arrived in northern Europe in the earliest days of the Christian era. It is known that the Germans were making a hops-flavored beer in the 11th century. By the 1200s, there was a thriving brewers' guild in Cologne (Köln).

In the earliest days of the beer trade, customers could not always be certain of the quality of the liquid they were drinking. In response, the German beer purity decree, the *Reinheitsgebot*, was promulgated in Bavaria in 1516. It simply listed certain price regulations and proclaimed the only ingredients allowed in the brewing process: barley, hops, yeast, and water. In 1906, the *Reinheitsgebot* became law, applying to all of Germany (but only for bottom-fermented, lager beers). The beer purity law is the world's oldest consumer-protection law still in effect.

German beers are brewed in many varieties. Lager beer's designation comes from the German word *lagern*, which means "to store." In the days before refrigeration, beer was usually brewed in the winter and stored for later consumption in the spring and summer—hence the term *lager*. In general, beer brewing is divided into two methods: top fermentation and bottom fermentation. The latter is used for lager beers and is an Austrian invention. Craft beer, an idea imported from America, is a growing trend in Germany, especially in large urban areas. In part, it is a reaction to Germany's beer monoculture.

In the table below, the Czech Republic continues its longtime lead in per person beer consumption. Namibia, a former German colony, rose from 5th place in 2015 to 2nd in 2016.

WORLD BEER CONSUMPTION—2015 (PER CAPITA)

1.	Czech Republic	143.3 liters
2.	Namibia	108.0 liters
3.	Austria	106.0 liters
4.	Germany	104.2 liters
5.	Poland	100.8 liters
6.	Ireland	98.2 liters
7.	Romania	94.1 liters
8.	Seychelles	90.0 liters
9.	Estonia	89.5 liters
21.	United States	74.8 liters
23.	Australia	71.4 liters
25.	United Kingdom	67.7 liters
34.	Canada	57.7 liters

Source: Kirin Beer University Report for 2016

Related Web links: bier.de—German beer site (G)

Munich's Marienplatz (square) is in the heart of Bavaria, a noted beer-drinking region.

The Basics of Dining Out

Dining out in Europe is not that different from doing so in North America, but there are a few key differences of which travelers and expats need to be aware.

Finding a Seat

Upon entering an Austrian, German, or Swiss dining establishment, do not wait to be seated. It could be a long wait. Diners are expected to find their own table. Sometimes one of the food servers may suggest a seat, but they are usually busy ignoring other customers who are already seated. If you see a sign that says (in German) "Please wait to be seated," you are about to pay way too much for your meal. But that is rare. Most of the time you just find your own seat.

Water

Probably because of Prohibition in the past, Americans expect a glass of water, suitably chilled, to automatically appear at their table in a restaurant. This is also the custom in Sweden, but not in Germany. If you want water, you'll have to pay for it, by the bottle—fizzy (*Sprudelwasser*) or plain (*stilles Wasser*); large (*groß*) or small (*klein*). Often the beer is cheaper. Trivia: Bottled seltzer water is a 1783 invention by a German-born Swiss man by the name of Jacob Schweppe. Today the Schweppes line of bottled water and tonic drinks carries on his name.

No Free Rolls or Ketchup

This does vary by restaurant, but the basket of rolls is usually not free. Ask if you're not sure. Even McDonald's charges extra for ketchup packs. Germans take the expression "no free lunch" seriously.

Paying and Tipping

The customary way of paying your bill and tipping is another area where North Americans can get confused. You pay for your meal at the table with your server. Unlike in the United States and Canada, not every restaurant in Germany accepts credit cards, especially if you stray from the tourist circuit, so always carry some cash. Tipping is not done the American way either. You never leave the tip (*Trinkgeld*) on the table. If paying cash, simply tell the waiter the amount you're paying, including the tip. If paying with a credit card, it's best to pay the tip in cash, otherwise the service staff may never see it. Note that, contrary to what some Germans will tell you, the tip is not included unless the menu or bill expressly states "inklusive Bedienung," which is rare. You should pay a normal tip of 10 to 15 percent (Germans often pay 5 to 10 percent), depending on the service you received. Of course, if the service was poor, you don't have to tip at all.

Related Web links: dehoga-bundesverband.de— website of the German hospitality association (G); **foodwine.com/destinations**—delicious guides to German and Austrian dining (E); **german-way.com**— many topics including dining out (E)

You *Can* Drink the Water—Just Don't Do It in Public!

The tap water (*Leitungswasser*, *Trinkwasser*) in Germany ranks among the healthiest in the world. However, most Americans who somehow learned the German phrase for "Tap water, please." ("*Leitungswasser bitte.*") rarely use the phrase a second time. The puzzled look of disgust on the server's face is usually enough to discourage all but the most emboldened diner from making any second attempt. It is a look that says: "Ordinary water is fine for bathing, but only a barbarian would drink it!"

Why don't Germans drink perfectly safe water? Theories on this topic abound, but the reasons for their reluctance—more like a phobia—may go back to a time when public water sources were truly hazardous to your health. This tap-water angst is not just a German thing, either. Most other Europeans also avoid drinking tap water—except perhaps accidentally when they brush their teeth—despite its high quality. German drinking fountains are a rarity.

If you want to see stares of disbelief and horror, just pour yourself a glass of water from the kitchen sink in front of your German hosts. Their expressions alone will tell you that you have just violated some cardinal rule of German culture. Your shocked German friends may tell you that tap water is for washing the dishes and bathing, not for drinking. In a restaurant, if you ask for water (and you do have to ask!), it will come in a bottle and will usually be carbonated, *mit Gas* (if you don't want carbonated water, ask for *stilles Wasser*).

Another reason for *Trinkwasser-Angst* is the taste of some local water. While there are exceptions, much of the water coming out of German taps, despite its safety, just doesn't taste that good. Often *das Wasser* may be hard and heavily calcified (*verkalkt*—also a derogatory term applied to people), another reason for the popularity of filtered or bottled water.

Although beer, wine, coffee, tea, colas, and even fruit juice are certainly popular with Germans, the biggest-selling beverage remains good old bottled *Mineralwasser* (mostly the sparkling version, *Sprudelwasser*). Germans drink more bottled water than any other beverage, including beer. While most of their European neighbors prefer non-carbonated (still) water, 76 percent of the bottled water Germans drank in 2016 was sparkling water.

World Mineral Water Consumption— 2016
European Mineral Water Consumption (per capita)

Italy	188.1 liters (*mostly still*)
Germany	175.4 liters (*mostly sparkling*)
Spain	126.3 liters (*mostly still*)
France	125.2 liters (*mostly still*)
Switzerland	114.0 liters (*mostly sparkling*)
Austria	91.6 liters (*mostly sparkling*)
U.K.	35.9 liters (*mostly still*)

Source: (2016): European Federation of Bottled Water; statista.com

---

Related Web links: **mineralwasser.com**—*Verband Deutscher Mineralbrunnen* (G); **wasser.de**—*Wasser.de* (G); **fruchtsaft.de**—*among other things, you'll learn that Germans drink more Fruchtsaft—fruit juice—than any of their European neighbors!* (G)

Germany's 50+ Regions

When most English-speaking people think of Germany, images of lederhosen, the Alps, Neuschwanstein Castle (the "Disney castle"), and Oktoberfest are usually the first things that pop into their heads. Of course, all of those things are Bavarian, not German. If you start thinking German cars (Audi, BMW, Mercedes, Porsche), you're still in southern Germany (except for Volkswagen in Wolfsburg). And then there's historical stereotype number one: Adolf Hitler—who was Austrian and liked to hang out in Bavaria. Bavaria is indeed part of Germany and is the country's largest state, but it is only one of 16 states (*Bundesländer*), and a state that has many regional differences within itself.

Germany is a nation of regions. Most of Germany's states were not even created until 1949, when the Federal Republic of Germany (West Germany) arose from the ashes of World War II. The German Democratic Republic (East Germany) came into existence at about the same time, but in 1952, it created 14 districts (*Bezirke*) and eliminated the former states. Only after reunification were the eastern German federal states restored.

Most countries have regional distinctions, and often a north–south divide. Germany is no exception. Its unofficial north–south border even has a name: *der Weißwurstäquator*, "the white-sausage equator" (or *die Weißwurstgrenze*, "the white-sausage border"). This rather loosely defined border is named for Bavaria's famed white sausage. One version is the linguistic Speyer line that roughly follows the Main River, dividing the Central German (north) and Upper German (south) dialects. Farther south is a more geographic version: a line running roughly along the 49th parallel, more or less along the Danube, or between the Main and the Danube rivers.

Most people who have never been to Germany, Austria, or Switzerland have no idea how regional those countries are. Germany has about 82 million people, most of whom have much more of a regional identity than a national (or a state) one. Germans live in regions with names such as Allgäu, Schwarzwald (Black Forest), Eifel, Franken (Franconia), Harz, Oberbayern, Ruhr (*Ruhrgebiet, Ruhrpott*), Rheinland, Schwaben (Swabia), and Taunus. There are over 50 different named regions in Germany, few of which correspond to the 16 states.

Unlike in the United States, Germans don't even use the state name in postal addresses! That's rather odd when you realize that there are three towns in three different German states named Königstein, or that there are a total of seven communities in Germany bearing the name Berg. It's a good thing there are *Postleitzahlen* (postal codes). Sometimes the region is added to the city name to clarify its location. A good example is Freiburg im Breisgau (Freiburg i.B.) in southwestern Germany in the state of Baden-Württemberg.

dastelefonbuch.de/Postleitzahlen—post code locator (G)

A Baedeker on Baedeker and German Wanderlust

The *Wall Street Journal*'s article on what was in and out in the "new economy" was subtitled "An After-Bubble Baedeker: How to Be Really Cool as the Economy Chills." That 2001 headline dates back almost exactly 200 years to the birth of Karl Baedeker (1801–59), the German publisher whose name has become a synonym for any guidebook or travel guide.

Baedeker is the name of a German publishing house (*Verlag*) founded in Koblenz by Karl Baedeker in 1827. The famous "Baedeker system" was first established when Baedeker published the second edition of a guide to the Rhine between Mainz and Cologne. In that 1839 guidebook, he established the formula of practical and reliable information, keeping the Baedeker travel publications popular to the present day—and helped spawn many imitators. In his Rhine guide, Baedeker also introduced the use of star symbols to indicate attractions of special interest. The combination of German wanderlust and detailed travel information allowed the Baedeker guides to develop a large market of travel-hungry readers. It was a pioneering stage in the development of what we now call "tourism" and the "travel industry."

Baedeker's father was a printer and bookseller when Karl came into the world in the city of Essen on November 3, 1801. Karl continued that publishing tradition and earned a reputation for honesty and reliability by personally visiting and checking up on the locations and hotels mentioned in his books. After his death, his three sons expanded the operation by covering foreign destinations and publishing French and English editions. The first Baedeker guidebook in English appeared in 1861. The Karl Baedeker Verlag has since been located in Leipzig, Hamburg, and now Freiburg in Breisgau. The firm continues to publish its guides, including the automobile guides (Baedeker Autoverlag) added in 1952.

The following are selected English-language Baedeker titles in 1911:

- *Austria-Hungary*, including Dalmatia, Bosnia, Bucharest, Belgrade, and Montenegro—10 marks ($2.50 U.S.)
- *The Dominion of Canada*, with Newfoundland and an excursion to Alaska—6 marks ($1.50 U.S.)
- *Palestine and Syria*, including the principal routes through Mesopotamia and Babylonia—12 marks ($3.00 U.S.)
- *The United States*, with excursions to Mexico, Cuba, Puerto Rico, and Alaska—15 marks ($3.50 U.S.)

(Note: Exchange rates are approximate and are based on the "Money Table" that appeared in the Baedeker guides in 1911.)

Related Web link: baedeker.com—Baedeker official site (G)

Ötzi and Andreas Hofer: The Mummy and the Martyr

The summer of 1991 is fading into autumn. High in the Alps of Südtirol—South Tyrol, the German-speaking region of northern Italy—at an icy spot on the Hauslabjoch (ridge) just 100 yards from the Austrian border, a German hiking couple make a gruesome discovery. Partially visible in the melting glacial ice is what appears to be a human body. When Austrian authorities arrived on the scene, at first they believed they were dealing with one more unfortunate mountain climber. After all, the *Gendarmerie* routinely recover the corpses of ill-fated climbers every summer. But, the frozen remains were astounding: the naturally mummified body of a Stone Age man who died 5,300 years ago.

Archaeologists and researchers would later be horrified over the brutal, unscientific extrication of the oldest intact human remains ever found. Nevertheless, the "ice man" and his earthly possessions continue to reveal much about how humans lived five millennia ago, shattering many previous theories in the process.

That startling Neolithic discovery made on September 19, 1991, on the Similaun Glacier reveals a lot about present-day regionalism and nationalistic sentiments. Ötzi (named for the Ötz Valley Alps where he died) immediately became the focus of a dispute between Austria and Italy.

One of the first concerns was which country had jurisdiction over the find. The bureaucratic custody battle continued, even after a binational survey team confirmed that Ötzi's remains had indeed been found on the Italian side of the border. In the meantime, Ötzi remained an Austrian resident—in a freezer at the University of Innsbruck. Finally, in 1998, with an armed military escort, the ice man was moved to his new Italian home in a $10 million museum built just for him.

Although the two countries eventually managed to reach an agreement, the process was complicated by several historical factors. One is the fact that the province of South Tyrol (Bolzano in Italian) is an autonomous region within Italy. Tyrol itself has long had an independent, strongly patriotic attitude—its citizens thinking of themselves more as Tyroleans (*Tiroler*) than Austrians.

As recently as the early 1960s, South Tyrolean activists were convicted of terrorist acts in an effort to take South Tyrol back from Italy and reunite it with North Tyrol (Nordtirol) and East Tyrol (Osttirol). Following World War I, the Treaty of Saint Germain ceded South Tyrol to Italy in 1919, despite a German-speaking majority in the region. Almost a century earlier, Andreas Hofer (1767–1810) became a Tyrolean martyr after Napoleon took him prisoner and ordered his execution after Hofer's success in battles against Bavarian and Italo-French forces. Today the *"Andreas-Hofer-Lied"* is the Tyrolean anthem.

Related Web links: iceman.it—for information on Ötzi (E, G); **museum.passeier.it**—for information on Andreas Hofer (E, G)

61

Berlin Bleibt Berlin: Berlin Will Always Be Berlin

Berlin stands under the sign of the pickax. In every nook and cranny of downtown, clouds of dust, ramparts of wheelbarrows, and placard-covered construction-site barricades proclaim that one structure is disappearing from the spot to make room for another. It is a never-ending process of rise and fall in modern Berlin. One could even speak of a demolition mania, were this tearing down not far removed from a vandalism that only destroys, and if it did not serve to replace the old with new towering buildings of greater luxury and usefulness through the more efficient use of space.
— BERLINER MORGENPOST

Although it sounds like a commentary about the German capital today, the newspaper excerpt quoted here first appeared in print on November 1, 1906. Over 100 years after it was written, the only thing needed to make this observation truly contemporary is to replace "pickax" with "bulldozer" and "wheelbarrows" with "construction cranes." Today's Berlin is one huge construction site.

Berlin has always been on the go. Since its early days as the Prussian capital, through its postwar division, and up to its renewed status as Germany's governmental center, Berlin has had an interesting and unique history. Even as a divided city, Berlin was a dynamic place, and few cities can claim a bigger role in modern world history. Today the German metropolis is once again taking on a truly metropolitan character befitting the largest city in the European Union's most populous country. In the 21st century, Berlin has the potential to rival other European capitals.

Not that the city is without any drawbacks. In a metropolitan beauty contest, Berlin would lose to most of its European competition. In many ways, Berlin is more a provincial gathering of small towns than a true metropolis. But then, that is also part of the city's charm.

Related Web links: berlin.de—official Berlin site (E, G); berliner-morgenpost.de—*Berliner Morgenpost*, newspaper online (G)

A Berlin Time Line

ca. 1200	Two trade settlements, Cölln and Berlin, arise on the banks of the Spree.
1432	Berlin and Cölln become one city: Berlin.
1806	Napoleon occupies Berlin for two-years.
1871	Berlin becomes the capital of the German Reich.
1945	The city is devastated by war and divided in two.
1948–49	Berlin Airlift takes place.
1961	The Berlin Wall is erected.
1989	Fall of the Berlin Wall; Germany is reunited.
1991	Berlin becomes the capital of reunified Germany.
1999	The renovated Reichstag is reopened.

Berlin's historical center and the Friedrichstraße Station were formerly in East Berlin.

Germany's Former Colonies

Germany's colonial overseas ventures were brief and ultimately unsuccessful. What started in Prussia under Otto von Bismarck in the 1880s ended in Kaiser Wilhelm II's Germany with the First World War (1914–1918). Few Germans are fully aware of their country's imperial past, but there are some surprises in Germany's overseas history.

1682 to 1721. Before the United States of America existed, Brandenburg and Prussia were involved overseas. In what is now Ghana, Groß-Friedrichsburg was the main town on Africa's "Prussian Gold Coast." In the Caribbean, the Prussians had outposts on Crab Island (*Krabbeninsel*, now Vieques, Puerto Rico) and on Saint Thomas, in today's U.S. Virgin Islands. By 1685, the Brandenburgisch-Africanische Compagnie was trading slaves in Africa and the Caribbean. But Prussia sold it all to the Danes and the Dutch. In the 19th century, Germany joined in the European grab for territory in Africa, the Pacific, and China.

German New Guinea. Prussian interest in the island of New Guinea began with trade in 1857. The black, white, and red German imperial flag was hoisted over *Deutsch-Neuguinea* in 1884. Three colonial powers—the Germans, British, and Dutch—shared the Pacific island. Bismarck claimed the northeast section and named it **Kaiser-Wilhelms-Land**. German New Guinea included Kaiser-Wilhelms-Land, New Pomerania, the Bismarck Archipelago, the northern Solomon Islands, the Caroline Islands, the Mariana Islands, the Marshall Islands, and a few others—until 1919. Only the "Bismarck Archipelago" and "Bismarck Sea" names remain on modern maps.

Cameroon (Kamerun). This "protectorate" on Africa's west coast was held by Germany from 1884 to 1919. Today, the Republic of Cameroon is an independent nation with two official languages: English and French.

German East Africa (*Deutsch-Ostafrika*). From 1885 to 1919, modern Rwanda, Burundi, plus parts of Kenya and Tanzania were a German colony. The Germans established an education system, and the Swahili word for "school" (*shule*) comes from German *Schule*.

German South West Africa (*Deutsch-Südwestafrika*). Today's Namibia, a nation twice as large as California, was a German colony from 1885 to 1915. The colonial history of Namibia represents a dark chapter in German history, including the first genocide of the 20th century and the first German concentration camps. The native Herero and Nama people were almost exterminated by German forces under Lt. General Lothar von Trotha. Germany has officially apologized for this crime, but has never paid reparations. Today, Namibia (capital: Windhoek, population: 326,000) is a prosperous, democratic nation with one of Africa's better economies. English is the official language, but Afrikaans, German, and several African languages are also recognized.

Tsingtao (Qingdao). German colonization in China was far less successful than the British in Hong Kong or the Portuguese in Macao, but they can claim one key achievement: The Chinese beer "Tsingtao" traces its origins back to German brewmasters.

The Alps (*Die Alpen*)

The mountains known as the Alps (*die Alpen*) cover four German-speaking countries and stretches across one-quarter of the earth from southeastern France all the way to Vienna. Its snowcapped peaks are sprinkled throughout the German-speaking countries of Austria, Germany, Liechtenstein, and Switzerland. The so-called Alpine Arc forms an 868-mile semicircle from Italy's Gulf of Genoa up through the German-speaking region where Italy and Austria border on each other (the Trentino-Alto Adige region in Italian, the province of Südtirol in German, Bolzano in Italian) and on across into Austria. The Alps are so long and varied that they are usually divided geographically into three sections: the Western, Central, and Eastern Alps. Geologists, however, tend to view the Alps as comprising two main sections divided by the so-called Rhine line, a north-south demarcation that runs through Lake Constance (Bodensee) down across the Septimer Pass just southwest of St. Moritz in Switzerland.

Western Europe's highest peaks are all found in the Alps, most of them in Switzerland. Although it is more famous, the Swiss-Italian Matterhorn tops out at only 14,690 feet, while Monte Rosa (15,203 feet), the Dom (14,911 feet), and the Liskamm (14,852 feet, in Italy and Switzerland) all are higher. The highest Alpine peak is Mont Blanc (15,771 feet), on the French-Italian border. Germany's highest peak is the Zugspitze, at 9,720 feet.

Of course, the Alps long ago gained fame as the prime location for winter sports, especially downhill skiing (*Abfahrtslauf*)—which was largely invented in the Austrian Alps and is also known as Alpine skiing, *alpiner Skisport*. (Cross-country skiing, *Langlauf*, comes from Scandinavia.) The Alps are dotted with famous ski resorts in every German-speaking country. Zermatt, situated at the base of the Matterhorn, is a legendary Swiss resort boasting the longest ski season in the Alps. Many Austrians and Swiss learn to ski about the same time they learn to walk.

The Alps are also a favorite for hikers, climbers, and *Sommerfrischler* (loosely, "summer fresh-air freaks"). A vast network of *Wanderwege*, or hiking trails, crisscrosses the Alps and the four countries they cover. There are 10 designated *Weitwanderwege* (long-distance trails) found in the Austrian Alps alone, from the Nordalpenweg (Rust am Neusiedlersee–Semmering-–Kufstein–Bregenz on Lake Constance) to the Rupertiweg (Bärnstein in the Böhmerwald–Salzburg–Königsee–Naßfeld in the Corinthian Alps). Even longer European trails run in both north-south and east-west routes across the continent, including the Alps.

Related Web links: slopes.waymarkedtrails.org—The Alps (E); **austria.info**—for walking & hiking suggestions (E); **hiking.waymarkedtrails.org**—for map and details of trails (E)

The German Health Care System

Health Insurance. Germany has the distinction of having established the world's first national health care insurance system—in the 1880s! The Prussian chancellor Otto von Bismarck established a basic health insurance program that at first covered only blue collar workers. Not known as a bleeding heart, the Iron Chancellor came up with his innovative health plan as a purely political move to counter the Social Democrats who had gained popularity in the *Reichstag* in recently unified Germany. To beat the socialists at their own game, Bismarck passed a law in 1883 that instituted mandatory, government-monitored health insurance. Funded by both employers and employees who paid into insurance funds (*Krankenkassen*), Bismarck's health insurance scheme, with various changes and improvements over time, is basically the same as that in effect today.

All German citizens—and foreigners living in Germany—are required to have health insurance. Whether you qualify for the public insurance system or private insurance depends on several factors. About 90 percent of the insured in Germany are in the public, statutory health insurance system (*Gesetzliche Krankenversicherung*, GKV). About 10 percent are privately insured, either because they are not eligible for public insurance or they earn more than €52,200 annually (subject to change) and opt to go private. All salaried employees are automatically enrolled in the public insurance plan, no matter the state of their health. If you are self-employed or a civil servant, then you must be privately insured, but private insurers can be more choosy about whom they accept, and the premium is higher than for public insurance.

Health Care and Causes of Death. Now let's compare how well the German system cares for the health of people living in Germany versus the U.S. health care system. First of all, medications, doctor visits, and hospital stays are cheaper than in the United States, while providing equal or even better care. Even without prescription insurance, most drugs are far less expensive in Germany than their U.S. equivalents.

While the top causes of death are similar in the two countries, Germans have a longer life expectancy (females, 83.3 years; males, 78.5 years) than U.S. Americans (females, 81.2 years; males, 76.5 years).[1] Infant mortality rates (deaths per 1,000 live births) in Germany (3.4) are far better than in the United States (5.8), Canada (4.5), and the United Kingdom (4.3). One measure of the quality and availability of health care related to mortality rates, the HAQ Index, rates Germany higher (86.4) than the United States (81.3).[2]

If you are a tourist in Germany, any non-German health or accident insurance you may have is not valid, but you usually can be reimbursed for any hospital or medical expenses you paid up front.

---

[1] 2016 data, **healthdata.org**
[2] 2015 data, 0–100, with 100 the best, **healthdata.org**

Killer Drafts and *Kreislaufstörung*: Germans and Their Favorite Ailments

Certain nationalities seem to fall prey to particular aches and pains. The French complain about their livers, Americans about their rheumatism, and Germans . . . well, Germans have a unique ailment of which few non-Germans have ever heard. Since the Germans long ago perfected the art of worrying in general, it should come as no shock that what they most often worry about is their health. And when they worry about their health, the most frequent concern is something called *Kreislaufstörung*, an amazing collection of circulatory ailments that can range from a headache to a heart attack. Indeed, it is difficult to find an illness that a German wouldn't classify as a *Kreislaufstörung* (circulation problem).

It is, in fact, this national preoccupation with *Kreislaufstörung* that in part led to Germany's spa tradition, a health-craze phenomenon that is rarely surpassed in any other culture. Taking the "cure" or the "waters" (*eine Kur machen*) is not only frequently prescribed by German doctors but also covered by German health insurance. The German language created the word *Kurort* (spa resort) just for places like Baden-Baden (spa-spa or bath-bath) that live off the German compulsion to take the waters. Of course, spas help with other non-*Kreislaufstörung* aches and pains (if there is such a thing), and Germans feel it is their right and duty to visit a spa at least once a year.

There is one more important German health concern of which any foreigner should be aware. The expression *es zieht* (there's a draft) will echo in your brain should you ever have the temerity to even slightly crack open a window on a hot summer day while on a moving train or in an automobile going more than five miles per hour. Germans and some other Europeans consider even the slightest breeze from an open window to be fatal! To the German mind, such a killer draft will surely lead to your demise from pneumonia or some other serious draft-related ailment. On certain German and Austrian streetcars, there are even signs admonishing passengers to not leave windows open. The whole thing gives an entirely new meaning to "avoiding the draft"! It makes one wonder just how Germany could possibly be the birthplace of the motorcar.

Kurort: Literally, "cure place," *Kurort* is an official designation for an area or resort specializing in the natural health remedies of mineral baths. German health insurance (*Krankenkasse*) covers these treatments. These places levy a special *Kurtaxe* on patients taking the cure. The term *Heilbad* or *Bad* (health spa, bath) is also an official one. Towns with *Bad* in their names are often also *Kurorte*.

Related Web links: baden-baden.de—*Baden-Baden* (E, G); rathen.de (G); bad-abbach.de (G); bad-griesbach.de (G); badsassendorf-online.de (G)

Das Rauchen: Smoking in Germany

For all their fanaticism concerning fresh air and healthy foods, Germans, Austrians, the Swiss, and Europeans in general are incredibly blasé about smoking. Although tobacco advertising on German radio and TV has been verboten since 1975, and passenger trains always had smoking and non-smoking cars, Germany was slow to introduce legal prohibitions on smoking in bars and restaurants, the workplace, and other public spaces. Although there were voluntary restrictions in some German hotels and restaurants beginning in the 1990s, the first official smoking bans did not appear before 2007.

Other than at airports (1990s), train stations (2007), and government offices, German federal law has little to say about smoking. All of Germany's 16 states have now introduced legal smoking bans, but they vary widely in scope and enforcement. Bavaria has some of the strongest anti-smoking laws. In August 2010, Munich invoked a smoking ban for Oktoberfest, a ban that continues today, although some tents offer separate smoking spaces.

It's not that Germany's smokers haven't been informed about the health risks of smoking. Since 2003, large, bold danger warnings have been printed on every pack of cigarettes. The cost of smoking in Germany has steadily increased over the years. The price of a typical pack of cigarettes was 3 euros in 2002. By 2012, a pack cost 5 euros. In 2017, a pack set smokers back 6.30 euros, of which almost 53 percent was the German tobacco tax. Sticker shock is one of the reasons why only 32 percent of Germans smoked in 2015, down from 38 percent in 2000, but still higher than in the United Kingdom and the United States in 2015: 20 percent.

Neighboring Austria has one of the highest smoking rates in the world, although it dropped from 46 percent in 2000 to 36 percent in 2015. Austria has been dragging its feet with regard to smoking restrictions for years. Enforcement is so lax that it's not unusual to see your Austrian server puffing on a cigarette behind the bar before bringing out your order. Fed up in February 2018, the Austrian Medical Association (ÖÄK) sponsored a petition against the right-wing government's attempt to eliminate a complete ban on smoking in the country's bars and restaurants. More than 100,000 Austrians signed it, forcing a debate.

Oddly enough, Germany had a better record on smoking during the Nazi era. Non-smoking Hitler and his government discouraged smoking in the workplace, and banned it in cinemas and schools. Tobacco advertising was restricted. One researcher estimates that some 20,000 German women avoided lung cancer because of "Nazi paternalism" that strongly discouraged women from smoking. In 1943, German scientists discovered smoking's lung cancer link and the dangers of secondhand smoke. But after the war their work remained largely unknown.

Related Web link: **rauchfrei-info.de**—Smoke-Free (G), **ni-d.de**—Nichtraucher-Initiative Deutschland (NID) (G)

Your Friendly *Apotheker*

One of the strengths of the German health-care system is the modest institution known as the *Apotheke*, the local pharmacy. If you are used to the convenience of buying nonprescription drugs and health-care products "over the counter" at any supermarket or drugstore, the first time you try to do this in Austria, Germany, or Switzerland will likely be a frustrating experience. It can't be done.

It seems odd that in the land where aspirin was invented it is difficult to obtain any. Even if you just want some aspirin, cold medicine, or other nonprescription painkiller, you will have to go to an *Apotheke* (apothecary shop). Just look for a big red "A" for *Apotheke*. Once there, you'll find that the German version of a pharmacy offers certain compensations for any loss of drug-buying freedom. The *Apotheker* serves as a combination doctor and pharmacist, filling a role that differs to a significant degree from the American counterpart.

A *Drogerie*, despite its name, isn't a drugstore. A *Drogerie* doesn't sell drugs or medicines. A German "drugstore" is more of a minimart for beauty products, toiletries, and detergents, but no medicines. Even in the *Apotheke*, you can't simply pick out a box of aspirin and pay for it. All the *Arzneimittel* (medications), prescription or not, are located behind the counter or in the back room. You may have to ask the *Apotheker* for something to treat a headache (*Kopfweh*). This person will then ask a few questions about what the problem could be and will soon come up with some appropriate *Medikament*. It's unlikely to be plain aspirin unless you insist on aspirin.

During nights and holidays, designated *Apotheken* stay open. Your doctor (*Arzt*) will usually tell you which pharmacy is open, but if you don't know, you can go to any nearby *Apotheke* and read the sign in the door that tells you the address of the one that is open that day. This information is also published daily in the local newspaper and sometimes online.

Your *Apotheker* can sometimes save you a trip to the doctor by giving you pharmacological advice. If you do not speak German, you should still do fine. Many pharmacists in German-speaking Europe speak English, or you can use sign language and pointing to indicate your particular problem if you don't have a German-speaking friend to help you. If you have a written prescription (*Rezept*) from a doctor, there is little difficulty.

Prescription Refills

If you require a certain medication and will be in German-speaking Europe for some time, it is advisable to take along a supply of the medication and a prescription for refills. A drug may be known in your home country by a different name from that in Europe. Some medications may not even be available at all in the other country due to different regulations. A sample may help determine the equivalent drug. The same advice is valid for eyeglasses and contact lens prescriptions.

The Captain from Köpenick: The Cobbler's New Clothes

In 1906, Wilhelm Voigt was a 57-year-old ex-con and ex-cobbler who would soon be known as the "Captain from Köpenick" (*der Hauptmann von Köpenick*). Following his release from prison, Voigt was caught in a catch-22 situation: in order to get a job, he needed a passport, but without a job he couldn't get a passport. Several attempts to secure a passport from the Prussian bureaucracy had not only proved fruitless but also led to his expulsion from Berlin.

In desperation, Voigt managed to procure a discarded Prussian captain's uniform from a secondhand shop. On October 16, 1906, he donned the uniform and assumed the role of captain (*Hauptmann*). He then commandeered a detail of soldiers, marched them to the town of Köpenick (now a district of Berlin), occupied the city hall, used forged orders to have the mayor arrested, and, to top it all off, made off with a strongbox containing about 4,000 marks from the town treasury. In a twist of irony, Voigt discovered that there was no passport office in the city hall.

After his own arrest and a two-day trial, Voigt was sentenced to four years in prison. In the meantime, the scoundrel shoemaker had become a folk hero in Prussia. Even Kaiser Wilhelm II was sympathetic enough to pardon Voigt before he had served half of his prison term.

The German playwright Carl Zuckmayer helped ensure that the Köpenick legend would live on. His *deutsches Märchen* (German fairy tale) dramatization of the event, starring some of the best actors of the time, had its premiere in Berlin on March 5, 1931. The Voigt story was also made into a German film in 1956, starring Heinz Rühmann.

Voigt's *Köpenickiade* (Köpenick escapade) cast both the Prussian bureaucracy and Prussian respect for the uniform over the man in a bad light. The "cobbler's new clothes" exposed the tendency of Germans to follow authority. Few true stories better illustrate the German maxim *Kleider machen Leute* (Clothes make the man). It was not only the Berliners who took a certain delight in Voigt's successful charade; his exposure of the stupidity of blind obedience and appearance over substance was a story that spread across Prussia and much of the rest of the world in 1906.

The real-life fairy tale had a relatively happy ending. Voigt, who had spent about 30 years of his life in prison, basked briefly in his Köpenick celebrity, even visiting the United States in 1910. He made enough money to manage a new start as a cobbler in Luxembourg, where he died in 1922.

In 1998, a life-size sculpture of Wilhelm Voigt, alias "Captain from Köpenick," was dedicated in the Berlin-Köpenick city hall. The long-overdue memorial, created by the Armenian artist Spartak Babajan, was installed in a ceremony that included a reenactment of the *Köpenickiade*.

Related Web link: **wild-east.de/berlin/koepenick /rathaus.html**—Köpenick-Rathaus, photo of the city hall in the distance and brief information about the Köpenick story (G)

Notable Women Yesterday and Today

Germany's best-known woman of today appeared suddenly on the international scene in November 2005, when she was elected Germany's first female chancellor. Since then **Angela Merkel** (1954–) has been reelected three times. In December 2015, *Time* magazine dubbed Merkel "Chancellor of the Free World" when it named her its Person of the Year, citing her resolve in leading Europe through the Greek debt crisis, and her encouragement of other countries to open their borders to migrants and refugees. But it was the refugee crisis in Germany itself that probably led to her lowest-ever victory margin in the 2017 national election, when she won her fourth term as chancellor. (For more about Merkel, see page 76.)

But other women have played important roles in German politics and many other fields, from cinema and fashion to business and science. They include:

Kirsten Dunst (1982–) German-American film actress: *The Bonfire of the Vanities* (1990), *Interview with the Vampire* (1994), *Jumanji* (1995), *Spider-Man* (2002), *Marie Antoinette* (2006), *Hidden Figures* (2016).

Cornelia Funke (1958–) Children's author (*Inkspell* series).

Nina Hoss (1975–) Film and stage actress.

Heidi Klum (1973–) German fashion entrepreneur, TV personality.

Diane Kruger (Heidkrüger, 1976–) German-American film actress: *Troy* (2004), *National Treasure* (2004), *Joyeux Noël* (2005), *Inglourious Basterds* (2009).

Ursula von der Leyen (1958–) Physician, politician, German Defense Minister.

Emmy Noether (1882–1935) Bavarian-born mathematician and theoretician. After gaining renown in Germany, the Jewish Noether was forced to leave Germany in 1933. She received a warm welcome at Bryn Mawr College in the United States, but died tragically only 2 years later of complications following the removal of a tumor.

Lilli Palmer (1914–1986) Film actress, writer; b. in Poznań, Poland. Films: *The Pleasure of His Company* (1961), *Miracle of the White Stallions* (1963), *Operation Crossbow* (1965), *The Boys from Brazil* (1978).

Amina Pankey (1983–), aka **Amina Buddafly**—German-American singer–songwriter, reality television star, and social media personality. Born in Hamburg.

Franka Potente (1974–) German film actress: *Run Lola Run* (1998), *The Bourne Identity* (2002), The Bourne Supremacy (2004).

Luise Rainer (1910–2014) German-born film actress who was the first to win two consecutive Academy Awards (*The Great Ziegfeld*, 1936; *The Good Earth*, 1937). Disillusioned with Hollywood, Rainer moved to New York, and later resided in London, England, where she died at the age of 104.

Sophie Scholl (1921–1943) Anti-Nazi student activist who, along with her brother **Hans Scholl** and several others in the White Rose movement, was executed for distributing anti-Hitler fliers in Munich.

Bertha von Suttner (1843–1914) Austrian-Bohemian pacifist and novelist; first woman to win the Nobel Peace Prize (1905).

Katarina Witt (1965–) Olympic ice skater

Related Web links: german-way.com/notable-people/notable-women—for concise biographies (E); iamamina.com—home page of Amina Buddafly (E)

Five Decades of Democracy

Turning 50 was a time for reflection in the Bundesrepublik. Just exactly when they should celebrate their country's 50th birthday was no certainty for Germany's citizens (*Bundesbürger*). The Federal Republic of Germany came into existence in a series of events that began with the introduction of the new Deutsche Mark currency in July 1948 and ended with the first session of the German lower house (*Bundestag*) and the formation of the country's first federal government (Bundesregierung) in September 1949. (In the eastern part of the country, another German republic, the Deutsche Demokratische Republik, had also been formed in 1949. If reunification had not ended its existence in 1990, the German Democratic Republic also would have celebrated its 50th birthday in 1999.)

But picking a specific date was the least of the problems connected with the German birthday celebration. As with almost anything German, the country's past colored even how it would commemorate its birthday. The horrors and excesses of the National Socialist (Nazi) era—which ended around the same time that the new Bundesrepublik began—gave "nationalism" a bad name in modern Germany. Although the radical right, skinheads, and neo-Nazis in today's Germany too often make the headlines, the vast majority of Germans are extremely uncomfortable with anything that smacks of nationalistic excess. German flag-waving is confined to team banners in soccer stadiums. If you look, it's difficult to even *find* a flag to wave. Not even many government buildings display the national flag.

There is no German equivalent of the American Independence Day celebration. (Firecrackers *are* heard in Germany, but mostly on New Year's Eve, *Silvester*!) How do you celebrate a nation's birthday when open patriotism is considered to be in poor taste? How do you celebrate a birthday when the country actually has several dates from which to choose?

Few Germans even know the date of their country's founding. It was on May 23, 1949, that the Federal Republic of Germany's Basic Law (*Grundgesetz*), or constitution, went into effect. But May 23 has never been a German holiday. How about November 9, the date of the opening of the Berlin Wall in 1989? No, too much heavy baggage from the Nazi *Kristallnacht* anti-Jewish pogroms that began on the night of November 9, 1938. So, German Unity Day (*Tag der deutschen Einheit*) is now celebrated on October 3, the official date of German reunification in 1990.

Related Web links: **bundestag.de**—German parliament (E, G); **bundesregierung.de**—German government (E, G)

Norman Foster's new glass dome atop the Reichstag is open to the public.

Alexander von Humboldt, the Famous German You've Never Heard Of

In the 19th century, Alexander von Humboldt (1769–1859) was as famous as Einstein was in the 20th century. News of his death on May 6, 1859, traveled around the world (slowly in those days) and saddened not only Germans (Prussians) but also people from Moscow to Buenos Aires.

The Prussian naturalist was born in Berlin. He would also die there almost 90 years later. Between his birth and death, Humboldt had trekked across much of the globe in a lifelong quest to answer questions about the geography, flora and fauna, and minerals on several continents. Though Humboldt the man is virtually unknown in the non–German-speaking world, Alexander von Humboldt's name is still very much with us.

The Humboldt penguin and Humboldt's lily (*Lilium humboldtii*) are just two examples of hundreds of animal and plant species bearing his name. Beyond our planet, the Humboldt crater and *Mare Humboldtianum* grace the moon, while the asteroid 54 Alexandra orbits the sun. One of the proposed names for a new U.S. western state was Humboldt, but it became Nevada instead. However, in Nevada today you will find Humboldt County (also in three other states), the Humboldt River, and the Humboldt Sink. There are Humboldt ranges in China, South Africa, and Antarctica. Humboldt Peak is found in Colorado's Rocky Mountains. The Humboldt Current in the Pacific Ocean flows northward along the western coast of South America.

Alexander von Humboldt's major, multivolume opus *Cosmos* was only partially completed before his death, but it could never have been written without the naturalist's adventurous, Indiana Jones–style scientific expeditions in Cuba, Mexico, the jungles of South America, and later in Russia's Siberian wilderness—all at a time when travel was far slower and much more dangerous and difficult than it is today.

On his way back to Europe from his South American expedition (1799–1804) with French botanist and physician Aimé Bonpland, Humboldt made a major detour via Washington D.C., the new capital of the United States of America. The explorer spent 6 weeks sharing information with the U.S. president, Thomas Jefferson, and other noted Americans. Having just completed the Louisiana Purchase, Jefferson was particularly grateful for Humboldt's detailed information concerning the new territory's border with New Spain (Mexico). They also eagerly discussed many other matters, but there was one topic Humboldt avoided discussing with the president: slavery. Jefferson was a slaveowner and Humboldt was very much opposed to any kind of slavery.

Unlike his older brother Wilhelm von Humboldt, a noted linguist, diplomat, and the founder of Berlin's first university, Alexander never married and preferred Paris over Berlin. But his scientific efforts helped make us more aware of the natural world and its vital forces.

Albert Einstein (1879–1955), the Genius from Swabia

The genius responsible for the theory of relativity that changed modern physics and how we think about time and space was born on March 14, 1879, in the Swabian city of Ulm in the state and kingdom of Württemberg in the German *Kaiserreich* (empire). But within a year of his birth, Albert's Jewish family moved to Munich in neighboring Catholic Bavaria. The family was not religious, and young Albert attended a Catholic elementary school and later a public secondary school in Munich. When he was 15, he left Munich before finishing high school. He promised his parents, now in Italy, that he would study to prepare for acceptance at the Zurich Polytechnic.

This early tendency to not stay long in any one place would continue for most of Einstein's life. At various times, Albert Einstein called the following cities home: Ulm, Munich, Pavia (Italy), Aarau (Switzerland), Zurich, Bern, Prague, Berlin (1914–1932), Caputh (summer house near Berlin), and Princeton (1933–1955). Einstein changed his citizenship numerous times, and for 5 years (1896–1901) he was stateless, a man without a country. In 1896, only 20, he renounced his German citizenship and applied to become a Swiss citizen, which he remained from 1901 until his death. Before also becoming a U.S. citizen in 1940, Einstein held Austro-Hungarian (1911–1912) and German (1918–1933) citizenship. Although claimed by several nations, Einstein preferred to think of himself as a citizen of the world.

Einstein spent only about 4 years in Bern, Switzerland, but they would be among the most important years of his life. This period included 1905, Einstein's *annus mirabilis* (extraordinary year), when he developed many of his key scientific theories, including the theory of relativity. He arrived in Bern in 1902 after securing a job in the patent office (Federal Office for Intellectual Property) there. Einstein married Mileva Marić in January 1903. Their first son, Hans Albert Einstein (1904–1973), was born in Bern in May 1904. (A mysterious unknown daughter, born earlier, has only recently come to light. She probably died around 1906.)

Although he had made his relativity breakthrough in 1905, Einstein did not receive the Nobel Prize for Physics until 1922, and it wasn't even for his theory of relativity, arguably his crowning achievement in physics! Einstein was traveling in Japan when the official Nobel awards ceremony took place in Sweden in December 1922, where he was granted the award for his "discovery of the law of the photoelectric effect." Oddly, Einstein would never receive a Nobel Prize for his relativity and gravitational theories.

The German-born physicist did indeed become a world traveler. Before fleeing the Nazis and settling in the United States, over the years Einstein had traveled to Paris, Palestine, Tokyo, New York, Chicago, Arizona's Grand Canyon, Pasadena, Berkeley (where his son Hans Albert was an engineering professor), Vienna, Salzburg, Brussels, Oxford, and many other places for conferences, causes, and family.

Angela Merkel and the Vladimir Putin Connection

Angela Merkel (*pron.* AHN-gay-luh MEHRK-ell) became Germany's first (and so far only) female chancellor on November 22, 2005. She has continued to serve in that office as the head of the Christian Democratic Union/Christian Social Union (CDU/CSU) for four consecutive terms, the latest beginning in March 2018.

Angela Merkel was born Angela Dorothea Kasner in Hamburg on July 17, 1954, but she grew up in East Germany, where she studied Russian, a required subject. Unknown to her, Leningrad-born Vladimir Putin, only 2 years older than Merkel, had considered German his favorite subject even before his posting to Dresden, East Germany, as a Russian KGB agent. He served there from 1985 to 1990, using the cover of translator. One of Putin's two daughters, Yekaterina, was born in Dresden in 1986. After the Berlin Wall fell, Putin returned to Leningrad (St. Petersburg after 1991). Merkel and Putin's paths first crossed in 2002, when Merkel met Putin in Moscow in her role as CDU leader. They both have been known to correct their interpreters' Russian or German during diplomatic meetings.

The year Angela was born, her father Horst Kasner (a Germanized version his Polish father's surname Kaźmierczak), a Lutheran pastor, was assigned to a church in the village of Quitzow in East Germany. Her mother Herlind (née Jentzsch) was a teacher of Latin and English. In 1957, four years before the Berlin Wall was erected, the family moved to Templin, about 50 miles north of Berlin. Angela Kasner, along with her brother Marcus and her sister Irene (both born in East Germany), thus grew up in the socialist Deutsche Demokratische Republik.

Angela attended school in Templin (Brandenburg) and studied physics at the University of Leipzig, graduating in 1978. She later earned her doctorate in quantum chemistry and pursued research in that field. Earlier, as a teenager, she was rewarded for outstanding proficiency in Russian with a free trip to Moscow.

In 1977 Angela Kasner married Ulrich Merkel, a physics student she had met during a Russian exchange trip, but they divorced in 1982. Her second and current husband is chemistry professor Joachim Sauer. They have no children, but Sauer has two grown sons from a previous marriage.

In the September 2017 federal election, the CDU/CSU won just 33 percent of the vote, its smallest share of the national vote since 1949. Angela Merkel found herself weakened and in unfamiliar territory, struggling to form a governing coalition. Martin Schulz's Social Democrats (SPD) at first declined to continue the GroKo "Grand Coalition," but after other protracted negotiations failed, "Mutti" (Mommy) Merkel was again in a red–black (SPD-CDU/CSU) coalition.

Related Web links: angela-merkel.de—Merkel's personal website (G); bundeskanzlerin.de—Official website of the German Chancellor (G)

Trautes Heim, Glück allein (Your Home Is Your Castle)

Germany has one of the lowest rates of home ownership in all of Europe. In neighboring Poland, more than 83 percent of residents live in a house or flat they own. Since its housing bubble crash in 2008, Spain has dropped from 85 percent home ownership in the late 1990s to about 78 percent in 2016, but the rate is still much higher than in Germany. The EU average in 2016 was 69.2 percent. France's 65 percent rate is slightly below that. The United States and the United Kingdom also had mortgage crises, but both now have home ownership rates above 63 percent. Austria comes in at 55 percent, but only 51.7 percent of Germans own their own home.

Why does Germany, with Europe's leading economy, rank near the bottom of the home ownership totem pole? There are three main reasons for this: (1) high prices, (2) tough mortgage requirements, and (3) a culture of renting. For the same reasons, the prosperous Swiss have an even lower rate of home ownership: 42.5 percent.

Starting with prices, as anywhere in the world, the cost of a house or condo (*Eigentumswohnung*) varies by location. Urban living is more expensive than living farther out in the country. A place in a small town will cost much less than in a big city. In early 2018, the average price of a house in Germany was €371,305.* A house of up to 100 square meters (100 m², 1,076 sq. ft.) cost €159,165; a larger place, with 180 m² (1,938 sq. ft.) or more cost €539,539. But a comparison of house or apartment costs by city in Germany reveals big differences.

Munich is Germany's most expensive city, whether you're renting or buying. The average cost per square meter (1 m², 10.76 sq. ft.) for a condo in Munich is €7,464. But in Munich's desirable Maxvorstadt university area, the average cost rises to €9,152 per square meter. Move north to Frankfurt am Main, and you'll pay an average of €5,701 per square meter to buy an apartment. In Swabian Stuttgart, the average cost drops to €5,025 per square meter. In the German capital of Berlin, the average is €4,557 per square meter, but the top price there is closer to €5,500 per square meter. Most German cities have a shortage of available housing, which puts upward pressure on prices.

The average price for a house in Frankfurt am Main is €931,583. The *average* in Munich's Schwabing district is €1.3 million! But the purchase price of a house or condo is only one hurdle. Lenders want no less than 20 percent down (40 percent is typical) plus fees and taxes. Although interest rates are low (2–5 percent), the terms are also shorter, 5 to 15 years, raising the monthly payment. A 15-year mortgage (*Hypotheke*) is considered a long-term loan in Germany. Fees and taxes can add another 12 to 15 percent to the total price.

*All housing prices by city are from immowelt.de (Feb. 2018, rounded to nearest euro).

Related Web links: A selection of nationwide real estate agents: **immobilien.de** (G), **remax.de** (G), **immowelt.de** (G), **engelvoelkers.com**—Engel & Völkers (E, G)

Advice on buying real estate in Germany: **web.allgrund. com/en** (E)

In der Küche: Everything but the Kitchen Sink?

The German word *Küche* means both "kitchen" and "cuisine." *Deutsche Küche* (German cuisine) is created in a German *Küche*. The kitchen in a German, Austrian, or Swiss home is usually smaller and more compact than its North American counterpart—not only because European homes and apartments themselves tend to be smaller, but also because European kitchen appliances are usually smaller and more economical. A typical German (or European) refrigerator (*Kühlschrank*) is about half the size of an American one. It therefore holds about half as much and uses half the energy. This is possible because traditionally, German homemakers shopped daily for groceries and therefore required less refrigerator space. Over the last two decades or so, though, Germans have been reducing the frequency of their grocery shopping to once or twice a week, making a larger *Kühlschrank* necessary. Of course, full-size refrigerators are available for those who prefer them and can afford to pay the higher purchase cost and the extra electricity charges.

If you are planning to buy or rent a German apartment, be aware that it may come with a "bare" kitchen. *Bare* is indeed the right word. Your new kitchen may be nothing more than four bare walls with roughed-in plumbing and electrical connections—even the kitchen sink may be missing! There are true stories of unsuspecting Americans moving into a new German apartment, only to end up doing the dishes in the bathroom sink (by candlelight) until they could install a new sink in the kitchen (and a bathroom light).

Once you have a kitchen sink (*der Ausguß, das Spülbecken*) in Germany, it will be missing something that is standard equipment in North American kitchens: an in-sink garbage disposal (*der Müllschlucker, der Küchenabfallzerkleinerer*). For environmental reasons, these devices have been outlawed in Germany since the 1960s. That situation could change, though. Because of advances in sewage treatment, there has been some recent discussion about possibly allowing garbage disposals to appear in German kitchens.

Related Web links: Kitchen appliance manufacturers: **aeg.de**—*AEG* (G); **miele.de**—Miele (G), **bosch-home.de**—Bosch, see *Products/Produkte* (E, G) Kitchen appliance retailer: **eichsfelder-moebelcenter.de**—Möbel (G)

Washing Machines Versus *Waschmaschinen*

Boil (*kochen*) or bleach (*bleichen*)? Top loader (*Toplader*) or front loader (*Frontlader*)? Short or long wash cycles? The debate about the alleged superiority of German/European washing machines versus American ones can reach a surprising intensity. German machines tend to be front loaders, while the American version is usually a top loader. Germans maintain that their washing machines clean far better than the North American equivalent.

Actually, independent comparisons indicate that both—whether top loader, front loader, European, or American—clean equally well. The real differences lie more in the area of economy (and ecology) and two distinct wash philosophies. Although Germans can buy top-loading machines, the great majority of European washing machines are front loading. (In North America, the situation is reversed.) Front-loading machines usually cost several hundred dollars more than top loaders, but they make up for this by being quieter and much more economical to run, using less water and energy.

German appliance maker Miele manufactured its first wooden tub muscle-powered agitator washing machine in 1901. Since then, Miele and other brands, with names such as AEG, Bauknecht, and Bosch, have gone on to be innovators in the field. The electricity and water consumption of European washing machines has been cut in half over the past 15 years, and there is now an EU (European Union) standard for all such appliances.

A North American using a German *Waschmaschine* (also called a *Waschautomat*) for the first time is in for several surprises. One of the biggest is the fact that a German machine often has a washing cycle as long as two hours! One Bosch machine has a wash program of 125 minutes but uses only 45 liters (11.8 gallons) of water per wash cycle. Compare that with one of the most economical U.S. front-loading models, which uses 103 liters (27 gallons) of water, or more than twice as much.

German *Waschmaschinen* also preheat the water to very hot temperatures (60 degrees centigrade, 140 degrees Fahrenheit), while U.S. machines use hot water from the water heater at 100 to 120 degrees Fahrenheit. Higher wash temperatures mean a German hausfrau has to use less bleach. Whites and cottons are usually washed at temperatures close to boiling (95 degrees centigrade, *Kochwäsche*). This, claim the environmentally conscious Germans, leads to less pollution, and since the washer heats only the water it needs, there is less energy consumption as well.

German machines also have high spin speeds (up to 1,600 revolutions per minute), which are more efficient in wringing most of the water out of the wash. Although most Germans hang the wash out to dry, those using a dryer use less energy because the clothes are better prepared for drying.

Related Web links: aeg.de—AEG (G); bosch.de—Bosch (E, G); miele.de—Miele (E, G); bauknecht.de—Bauknecht (G)

The Garbage Police

Few countries in the world are as picky about their waste as Germany is. Many German communities, large and small, even have special websites to explain all the variations and requirements for garbage day.

In Germany, you don't just toss anything at random into the garbage pail or wastebasket. Almost every community has strict rules about *Mülltrennung*, or waste separation, and garbage collectors are strict about those rules. If you have mixed your glass waste with the *Bioabfälle* (biodegradable waste), neither will get picked up. Certain waste categories are collected less or more frequently, and there are separate containers for each one, designated by labels and differing colors.

The *Biotonne* (bio can) is strictly for biodegradable waste. According to the online garbage guidelines for the city of Heilbronn, biodegradable waste makes up about 40 percent of household waste. Such waste is now composted by the waste authority, and a separate *Biotonne* is required. What can't go into the bio can? ". . . disposable diapers, sanitary napkins, fluid food waste, vacuum bags, ashes, cigarette butts, sweepings, plastic bags, drink cartons, textiles, leather, wool, layered paper, brochures." Only food leftovers, eggshells, hair, paper napkins, grass cuttings, and the like are allowed. During most of the year, *Biotonne* pickup is every 14 days. Only during the months of June, July, and August is biodegradable waste collected weekly.

The "Yellow Sack" (*Gelber Sack*) or yellow container is intended for disposal of packaging materials, including foil, plastic, aluminum cans, and plastic bottles. Used paper, cardboard, and glass do *not* go into the yellow container; they need to be placed in special collection containers for recycling. There are also special rules for the disposal of batteries, household and/or hazardous chemicals, building materials, *das Recyling*, and other categories.

Mannheim's online "*Abfall von A–Z*" ("Waste from A to Z") stresses the avoidance of waste in the first place. It promotes the two Vs: *Vermeiden und Verwerten* (avoid and process). The Mannheim guidelines say that you should think about garbage when you shop: "Therefore you should avoid items with too much packaging as well as throwaway products." The directive then goes on to give half a dozen suggestions for avoiding waste. One of these tips is something that many Germans do anyway: take along your own shopping bag and avoid plastic disposable bags (for which most German stores charge extra).

Related Web link: abfallratgeber.heilbronn.de—
Heilbronn Online, *Abfallratgeber Haushalte* (waste adviser) (G)

Kehrwoche: Your Turn to Sweep!

Swabia is a fuzzily defined linguistic and historic region in southwestern Germany, lying mostly in Baden-Württemberg in the area around Stuttgart and Tübingen. Swabians are known for being thrifty and neat, so they invented a system that incorporates both virtues: *Kehrwoche*, or "sweep week."

Kehrwoche can involve much more than a bit of sweeping. The whole idea is to share the chores of keeping the common areas—stairways, walkways, vestibules, and such—clean and tidy. And safe, as in winter, when an icy sidewalk could become a problem, or in the fall, when wet, slippery leaves can pose a hazard.

The system varies from place to place, but generally you will spot a so-called *Kehrwoche-Kalender*—a schedule of when which residents have the *Kehrwoche* responsibilities. Sometimes the landlord sends out a printed notice to all tenants in the building, while other apartment houses place a "*Kehrwoche*" sign next to the door of the designated apartment for that week. In any event, tenants who do not carry out their cleaning duties, or don't do them to the degree expected, can be subject to withering looks or outright snide comments.

Just what happens during *Kehrwoche*? If this is your first time dealing with "sweep week," it's a good idea to observe what your fellow apartment dwellers do. Most apartments have a list of duties, and in most cases your *Kehrwoche* obligations are even stipulated as part of your rental contract. Except during the winter season, usually the main thing is to sweep and mop the stairs, landings, entryway, and other common areas.

In winter, the sidewalks should be shoveled and sanded. (Salt is usually frowned on or even illegal. Shoveling snow on walks is sometimes optional.)

Knowing all this, you may wish to consider an apartment building with contracted cleaning services. Larger apartment complexes usually do not have *Kehrwoche*. The minus side is that such apartments may be more expensive than those where the tenants do the dirty work. Before you sign that rental contract, make sure you know whether you'll have janitorial duties or not!

In 1988, when Stuttgart changed the city ordinance requirement to sweep the sidewalks "mindestens einmal wöchentlich" (at least once a week) to "bei Bedarf" (when required), many locals protested, viewing the change as a threat to cleanliness and order. There is no overall legal obligation in Germany, but Kehrwoche may still be an enforceable part of a rental contract.

Gartenzwerge—German Garden Gnomes

Long before the Travelocity roaming gnome, with his white beard and pointy red hat, Germans were fond of their *Gartenzwerge*. The colorful, chubby-cheeked ceramic or PVC statues adorn many of the country's front yards and gardens. Despite being viewed by many Germans as *kitschig* (tacky, kitschy) and the equivalent of plastic pink flamingos, the garden gnome has proved to be an enduring German phenomenon that thrives on the German love of gardening, ties to Germanic mythology, and the need to stake out territory.

But just how typically German is the garden gnome? Its origins go back far in time, but the oldest preserved stone dwarves are 28 baroque marble figures designed in the 1690s by the Austrian architect Johann Bernhard Fischer von Erlach for the *Zwergelgarten* ("gnome garden") at the Mirabell Palace in Salzburg. Later, more baroque gnomes would appear in palatial gardens in what are today Austria, Germany, northern Italy, and Slovenia. Few of them remain today, as garden gnomes fell out of favor with the nobility by the early 1800s. But they would soon regain popularity in the more bourgeois stratas of society in Germany, England, France, and other parts of the world.

In 1872, in the Thuringian town of Gräfenroda, in what is now eastern Germany, two firms began manufacturing terracotta garden gnomes. The two workshops run by August Heissner and Philipp Griebel were soon mass producing their fired-clay creations. By 1898, the Gräfenroda gnomes were being sold at the Leipzig trade fair. Soon there were many firms cranking out garden gnomes for the domestic and foreign markets. Philipp Griebel's descendants are still producing garden gnomes, the last remaining producer in Gräfenroda.

Things slowed down only during two world wars. Following the creation of the German Wine Road (*Deutsche Weinstraße*) in the Palatinate in 1935, a Nazi *Gauleiter* condemned garden gnomes as a "disturbing disruption" of the landscape, and even banned them on private property. After the Second World War, garden gnomes saw a resurgence in popularity in Germany and Europe. By the 1970s, more humorous types of gnomes, departing from the staid, traditional designs, again boosted the popularity of the statuettes. In the 1980s and 1990s, traveling gnome pranks became popular. This fad was later reflected in the 2001 French film *Amélie*, starring Audrey Tautou, in which Amélie steals her father's yard gnome and gives it to a stewardess friend who takes it around the world and mails back pictures of it from famous places to show him what he is missing in life.

In the 1990s, German gnome makers faced growing competition from cheap knockoffs made in Poland. Many Bavarian and other German gnome firms were forced out of business. Only after Poland became a member of the European Union were they able to recover, but today most German garden gnomes are made of PVC plastic. These cheaper versions can cost as little as 20 euros, compared to ceramic gnomes priced from 35 to 80 euros, depending on size and design. Today there are an estimated 25 million garden gnomes in Germany.

Related Web link: zwergen-griebel.de/shop/index.html— Philipp Griebel in Gräfenroda (G)

Doors and Locks

German doors and locks are an indication of the German obsession with privacy. Doors, exterior or interior, are sturdy, well-crafted barriers to intrusion. In homes and offices, doors are numerous and more likely to be closed than open. An open-door policy is a rarity in Germany.

To keep them closed, German locks are made to standards that are equal to or better than the doors they secure. They are an imposing construction of tumblers, pins, shafts, bolts, and double-locking mechanisms with keys to match—a locksmith's dream and a burglar's nightmare. Outside door locks are almost always double-locked affairs that require a special course just to learn how to use them.

The Romans invented metal locks, but German locksmiths, particularly in Nürnberg in the Middle Ages, are credited with improving the devices. More modern improvements, including the American Yale lock and the more recent Swiss Kaba lock, are refinements of the ancient Egyptian wooden pin-tumbler lock. The Kaba lock features a smooth-sided key with dimplelike depressions, unlike most keys, which usually have serrated, grooved sides.

Increasingly, German hotels, especially upscale ones, are using computer-coded locks with magnetic key cards.

Along with substantial fences, thick hedges, roll-down metal shutters (*Rolladen*), iron gates, double-paned windows, and other spatially defining constructions, the German door commands respect and maintains the privacy of its owner. Behind that closed door, Germans can count on comfort and privacy. It serves both to keep things out (noise, people) and to keep things in (warmth, a secure feeling).

Traditionally, a German door kept in the warmth when only one room of the house was heated in winter. Today, despite central heating, every room, even in a small apartment, has a door with lock and key. In an office building, doors serve to keep out the noise from corridors and fellow workers.

All those doors help serve to separate and define Germanic space. Like a medieval castle, a German home or office has clearly defined compartments. Many Germans are confused by modern open-space offices that lack those solid divisions.

Related Web links: fsb.de—FSB-Klinken, a German maker of door latches (E, G); **hewi.com**—HEWI, a German maker of door latches (E, G)

Crime in Germany

As in most other countries, the German crime rate varies by location and from year to year. In 2016, after many years of holding the dubious honor as Germany's most crime-ridden city, Frankfurt am Main was finally able to shift its "crown" to Berlin. In fact, with a rate of 15,671 reported crimes per 100,000 population, Frankfurt fell to fourth place in Germany's ranking of cities with a population of 200,000 or more (after third-place Leipzig and second-place Hannover). Berlin's crime rate was 16,161 per 100,000.

As in the United States, the overall German crime rate has actually fallen over the past two decades. For example, in 1998 Frankfurt recorded 19,128 crimes per 100,000, amounting to a reduction of 3,457 (–18%) over 18 years (1998–2016). Even Berlin's figures represent an improvement. While the capital city has grown, crime has not. However, one thing has remained constant in Germany: the north–south divide in crime statistics. In general, states and cities in Germany's south have a lower crime rate than in the north. The average for Germany is 7,755 per 100,000. The averages in Baden-Württemberg and Bavaria in the south are 5,599 and 6,871, respectively. Munich (7,909) and Augsburg (7,988), both in Bavaria, had the lowest crime rates for large German cities, less than half of Berlin's rate and below the national average.

Murder. Crime rates in Germany are comparable to those in most Western countries, including the United States, but when it comes to violent crimes, including murder and manslaughter, Germany is far safer than the United States. The murder rate per 100,000 people in the United States was 5.3 in 2016. Germany's rate was 0.85 in 2015. The safest city in the United States was San Diego, which had a total of 50 murders, or 3.5 per 100,000 in 2016. Berlin had 92 homicides in 2016, a rate of 2.6 per 100,000.

Germany's official statistics may not always provide an accurate accounting of the level of crime. By one estimate from the head of the German Detectives Union (BDK), only about 75 percent of domestic burglaries were reported, and sex crimes and cybercrimes were underreported.

Incarceration Rates. This is a category in which the United States leads the world. Germany, which like all EU nations has no death penalty, had an incarceration rate of 77 per 100,000 population in 2016, lower than France (101) and neighboring Austria (94). The U.S. rate in 2015 was 666 per 100,000, with a total prison population of 2.15 million. Canada's rate per 100,000 was 114 that year.

Related Web links: **bka.de**—*Bundeskriminalamt* (G); **prisonstudies.org**—worldwide incarceration stats (E); **ucr.fbi.gov**—FBI Uniform Crime Reports, for U.S. figures (E)

The Police in Germany: *die Landespolizei*

The term *Landespolizei* refers to the normal, everyday police agencies based in each of Germany's 16 states. Each *Land* today has its own police force, ranging from 3,600 police officers and staff in Saarland to 42,000 in Bavaria.

German law and German law enforcement have evolved over the centuries from feudal times to Prussia, the Weimar Republic, and the Nazi era. Present-day German police forces were originally set up as part of an Allied effort to restore democracy to Germany after World War II. Reacting to the centralized, all-powerful Nazi police state that ruled Germany until 1945, a new way of policing was written into the *Grundgesetz*, the constitution of the Federal Republic of Germany. The result is a largely decentralized system under which each of the *Bundesländer* has primary responsibility for administering law enforcement at the local and state level. Although, as in the United States, there are police agencies at the federal level (see p. 86), everyday, normal law enforcement, from handing out traffic tickets to solving murder cases, falls to the police forces at the state level. In most cases, the police agencies have the following divisions:

Schupo, Kripo, and LKA. The *Schutzpolizei* ("protection police," *Schupo*) division handles public safety, general law enforcement, and traffic enforcement. The *Kriminalpolizei* (*Kripo*) division is concerned with the prevention and enforcement of criminal offenses. Every state also has a *Landeskriminalamt* (LKA), a state bureau of investigation, that works with the *Kripo* to investigate and solve crimes at the state level. The LKA also works with the federal *Bundeskriminalamt* (BKA) when cases extend beyond state jurisdiction.

Verkehrspolizei/Autobahnpolizei. The organization and structure of the traffic police or highway patrol varies from state to state. Some states do not have a separate *Autobahnpolizei*, leaving that responsibility to the regular *Verkehrspolizei* (traffic police), who also police trucking.

Police Colors. Beginning in 2005, Germany's police forces began to conform to EU standards for police uniform colors, moving from the traditional forest green jackets and beige pants to navy blue. Hamburg was the first state to make the change, along with the *Bundespolizei*, and soon other states followed—slowly. Now all German (and Austrian) police have made the switch to blue. Even in Bavaria, one of the last holdouts, the police began testing more stylish dark blue uniforms in 2015. All across Germany, police vehicles have also changed from a green-and-white/silver color scheme to blue and silver, but even over a decade after the changes began, a mix of old and new vehicle colors still can be seen in some locations.

Related Web links: bayern.de/polizei—Polizei Bayern, Bavarian police force (G); **polizei.berlin.de**—Berlin police force (E, G) (Most of the German *Länderpolizeien* have similarly addressed sites.)

Local police forces (sample): **justiz.bayern.de**—*Bayerisches Staats-ministerium der Justiz*, Bavaria's ministry of justice (G); **duesseldorf.polizei.nrw**—the Düsseldorf police website (E, G); **polizei.gv.at**—Austria's police (G); **polizei.ch**—Swiss police (G)

The Federal Police in Germany: *Bundespolizei* and the BKA

As noted previously, the German law enforcement system is largely decentralized, with most police powers delegated to Germany's 16 *Länder*. The two main exceptions to this state model are the *Bundespolizei* (BPOL, Federal Police) and the *Bundeskriminalamt* (BKA), both operating at the federal level. A third federal police agency, the *Polizei beim Deutschen Bundestag* (German Bundestag Police) is limited to protecting the members and staff of the German parliament in Berlin.

The BKA, headquartered in Wiesbaden, is similar to the U.S. Federal Bureau of Investigation. While not as glamorous or as well known as the FBI, the BKA plays a similar role in German law enforcement. It maintains Germany's central police archives, supports local law enforcement efforts, coordinates activities at the international level (Interpol, Europol, and foreign police authorities), protects officials of the German federal government, investigates certain types of crimes (international terrorism, threats against federal officials, and so forth), works with the state LKA units, and is responsible for witness protection. The BKA also maintains a central DNA database for all of Germany's police forces.

The BKA trains its own agents and officials in a 3-year program at the *Fachhochschule des Bundes für öffentliche Verwaltung* (Federal Academy for Public Administration) and also helps train other police personnel, especially in the areas of forensics and DNA analysis.

Established in 1951, the BKA has seen its responsibilities increase over the years. In addition to new offices in Berlin and Meckenheim bei Bonn, more buildings were was added in Wiesbaden to house a growing staff. In 2006, the BKA was given new antiterrorism mandates, including working with state authorities and setting up an antiterrorism database.

The *Bundespolizei* grew out of the former paramilitary *Bundesgrenzschutz* (BGS, Federal Border Guard) originally formed as a response to the epic failure to rescue 11 Israeli hostages during the 1972 Olympics in Munich. The BGS became the *Bundespolizei* (BPOL) under the *Bundesministerium des Innern* (Federal Ministry of the Interior) in 2005. The Federal Police now do essentially the same job as the former BGS, but under a new name. BPOL's job includes guarding airports and train stations, acting as sky marshals, protecting federal buildings, controlling non-EU borders, protecting German embassies abroad, handling asylum-related matters, providing counterterrorism forces (via the GSG 9 special unit), coast guard (*Küstenwache*) patrols, and backing up state police forces when requested. The BPOL has about 41,000 personnel, including 30,000 trained police officers. National headquarters (*BPOL-Präsidium*) are in Potsdam, and there are eight regional centers (*BPOL-Direktion*).

Related Web links: bundespolizei.de—German Federal Police, BPOL (G); bka.de—Bundeskriminalamt (BKA) official site (G); bka.de/EN—BKA, English summary of German crime statistics, check for Current Information (E); bundesgrenzschutz.de—Bundesgrenzschutz official site (G)

LANGUAGE

German in Germany: What You Don't Know Can Hurt You

Spending time in Germany, especially a long-term stay, without knowing anything about the language is not only foolish but also frustrating. Beyond the fact that life will be more fun and interesting, and you'll be more effective, speaking German is simply the courteous thing to do. It will also help reduce embarrassment and confusion.

But you probably have some good excuses for not learning German: German is too difficult. (Really? What if you were in Japan, Russia, or Greece—with a totally different alphabet?) People always want to speak English with me. (Could that be because your German is so poor?) I don't have the time. (No, you just don't want to make time.) You know how people in the United States or Britain complain about foreigners not learning English, not fitting in? You are now that foreigner.

First, a few examples of why you should learn German, and then we'll point out some ways to do that. Do you know what a *Stammtisch* is? Besides being one way to learn German, it's a table reserved for regular customers or a special group. You may know that *Ausgang* means exit, but *Notausgang* does not mean "not an exit." It's an emergency exit. *Einstieg* tells you which end of the bus or streetcar to board. *Hochspannung* is high voltage that could kill you. German has more than one word that means "you." Using the wrong one can lead to problems. You can learn more about *du, ihr,* and *Sie* in the "Daily Life and Customs" section.

If you want to learn German, there's really no better place for that than Germany. But if you aren't yet in Germany, you should get a head start by learning as much as possible before you arrive.

- **Goethe-Institut** This worldwide cultural and language organization is supported by the German government. It is highly rated but also costly. If there's not one nearby, their online courses are cheaper.
- **Volkshochschule (VHS)** The public "people's college" is an adult evening school for German and other subjects. Found in almost any German city of moderate size, the VHS (fow-hah-es) has the advantage of low cost and meeting other foreigners learning German. Some are better than others.
- **Stammtisch/Language Exchanges** Free or low-cost groups that meet to improve their language skills. Native-speaker volunteers offer authentic German.
- **Private Language Schools** If you're in a large city, you'll have many options. It pays to compare and get reviews. The better ones have small classes, but also may have a waiting list.
- **Apps/Online** This option has improved over the years. Some are better for beginners (Babbel), while others (Yabla) are for advanced learners. Some use Skype for a face-to-face experience.

Related Web links: thoughtco.com/german-4133073—German language (E,G); **goethe.de**—The Goethe Institute offers language courses for foreigners, both in Germany and in various other countries around the world (G, E)

False Friends and Imposters

The similarities between English and German can be risky. Many German words can be "false friends"—words that seem to be something they are not. Linguists refer to them as "false cognates" because they appear to be the same as their English relations, but they can mean something altogether different in German. Their misuse can cause problems ranging from mild amusement to extreme embarrassment. English speakers should be aware of the following common German "false friends":

- *aktuell* = up-to-date, current, present ("actual" is *echt or wirklich*; "actually" is *eigentlich*)
- *also* = thus, therefore (English "also" is *auch* in German)
- *das Argument* = a reasoned argument or point, usually not a disagreement (*der Streit*)
- *bald* = soon
- *Billion* = trillion (an American "billion" is *eine Milliarde* in German)
- *Box* = speaker for a stereo system; electrical or telecommunications junction box
- *die City* = the downtown city center of a larger town (although it sometimes equals *Stadt* (town))
- *der Dom* = cathedral (a "dome" is *eine Kuppel*)
- *das Etikett* = label, sticker, tag ("etiquette" is *die Etikette* or *Anstandsregeln*)
- *Evergreen* = an old musical standard, a classic popular song (not trees)
- *fast* = almost
- *der Fotograf* = photographer (a "photograph" is *ein Foto*)

- *die Garage* = garage of a house (a garage for repairs is called *eine Autowerkstatt*)
- *das Gift* = poison (a "gift" or "present" is *ein Geschenk*)
- *das Gymnasium* = high school, secondary school (a "gym" is *eine Turnhalle* or *Sporthalle*)
- *konsequent* = consistent ("consequently" is *folglich* or *als Folge*)
- *das Menü* = today's special in a restaurant (a "menu" is *eine Speisekarte*)
- *der Oldtimer* = an antique car (not used for people)
- *Reformhaus* = health food or natural food store
- *See* = sea (*die See*) or lake (*der See*)—the gender of the word makes all the difference!
- *Slip* = briefs; underwear that just slips on and off (a woman's "slip" is *das Unterkleid* or *der Unterrock*)
- *Slipper* = loafer, shoe without laces (a "slipper" is a *Pantoffel* or *Hausschuh*)
- *Warenhaus* = department store; also called *ein Kaufhaus* (a "warehouse" is a *Lagerhaus*)

Related Web link: thoughtco.com/
german-vocabulary-4133068 (E)

Preserving the Language: Is It German, English, or Gernglish?

That German talking on his *Handy* (cell phone) is using the CityRate while standing in line at the post office to send a Pack-Set. Many Germans take out a BahnCard to purchase a train ticket for the high-speed InterCity Express (ICE). Germans used to watch *Fernsehen*, a word that has largely given way to *TV* (but at least they pronounce it TAY-FOW). A bestselling German television program guide is named *TV Today*, and the country's number two newsweekly is called *Focus*. (Number one *Der Spiegel* has not yet changed its name to "The Mirror.") The German movie magazine with the biggest circulation bears the title *Cinema*.

Although the English invasion of German has been going on for a long time, some Germans are becoming concerned about the recent barrage of "Gernglish."

The worst *Wortpanscher* (word dilutor) offenders are advertisers. A recent German magazine ad for the U.S. television series "Stargate SG-1" contained more English than German, including the slogan for its beer company sponsor: "The International Taste." Three sentences in a Samsung ad for television sets are in German, but the ad ends with an English slogan: "Challenge the Limits." An ad for Europcar (itself an English name) claims in English: "You rent more than a car." Acer, a British computer firm, splashes across a two-page ad in large yellow letters: "Know How! No Risk! (*Das Knowhow* has been a common "German" word for years.) *Natürlich alles*, including *das* Business Notebook or *der* Miditower, will be configured for you in a "just in time" manner! Ads for the Siemens pocket reader claim it is the world's first "Offline-Textreader."

Despite a report stating that German consumers were put off by English advertising slogans, many German and international companies don't seem to think so. They use English phrases and expressions in their messages to consumers in Austria, Germany, and Switzerland.

Some critics of German "language dilution" have become alarmed enough to ask, "*Gibt es eine Krise der deutschen Sprache?*" ("Is there a German language crisis?") But others point out that German, like most languages, has survived similar linguistic invasions. Historically, both Latin and French have had a powerful impact on German. Such defenders of "English enrichment" are not concerned about German's survival and remind people that during the 17th and 18th centuries French had an even greater influence on German than English does today.

Nevertheless, the Verein Deutsche Sprache (VDS, German Language Association) battles on as the defender of the language. However, when they complain about the new English term for restrooms, *WC Center*, driving out the old word *Toilette*, VDS members ignore the fact that *Toilette* is French, not German.

Related Web links: **acer.de**—*Acer Corporation's German site* (E, G); **vds-ev.de**—Verein Deutsche Sprache (German Language Association) is a group that tries to defend German against English (G); **compaq.de/produkte**—*Compaq Germany site* (G)

German Spelling Reform (*Rechtschreibreform*) and the ß

German orthography (*Rechtschreibung*) has undergone several changes over time, with the most recent reforms in 1901, 1996, and 2006.

The first-known written versions of the German language date from the 8th century. At that time in Europe, Latin was the language of the church and academia, but the Latin alphabet proved inadequate to the task of capturing certain German sounds. Over the next few centuries German developed new letters and features to better reflect the spoken word. The *Umlaute* (ä, ö, ü) began as a, o, and u with an "e" written above them. Over time the e became two dots, adding three new letters to the German alphabet—and keyboard.

A unique feature of the German alphabet is the ß character, found in no other language. Until recently, part of the uniqueness of the ß, aka "es-zett" ("s-z") or "scharfes s" ("sharp s"), was that, unlike all other German letters, it existed only in the lower case. In a language that loves capitalization, there was no capitalized version of the ß, probably because it never appears at the beginning of a word. But in all-caps situations (as in HEADLINES), the ß had to be represented by SS (preferred) or SZ. See the example of the new letter here.

ẞ

Its use had been discussed since the late 19th century, but the capitalized ß (ẞ) did not make its official debut until June 2017—and not everyone was pleased. The uniqueness of the ß may help explain why many Germans and Austrians are so attached to it—and why they don't like to see it altered in any way. Part of the 1996 reforms involved discontinuing the use of the ß in many (but not all) words.

Although the Swiss have somehow managed to survive without the ß in printed or written Swiss German for decades, many non-Swiss writers, editors, and publishers were soon up in arms over its possible demise. While Germans and Austrians were driving down a **Straße** (**STRAßE**, street, road), the Swiss were perfectly content with a **Strasse** (**STRASSE**).

A few examples of German ß-words that changed in the 1996 reform (old form in parentheses):

- *dass (daß)*—that
- *ein bisschen (ein bißchen)*—a little bit
- *hässlich (häßlich)*—ugly
- *Schloss (Schloß)*—palace, castle
- *er isst (er ißt)*—he eats

There were many other spelling changes, too numerous to list here. When in doubt, check your *Duden*, in print or online.

Related Web link: duden.de (Duden is the authority on German spelling)

Language Borrowing: Denglish

Languages are always borrowing words from each other. English has adopted and adapted many words from French, German, and other languages. German immigrants and other sources have enriched English with numerous words of German heritage. Young children attend a kindergarten (children's garden). At Christmas, they eagerly await Kriss Kringle (a corruption of *Christkindl*, the German giver of Christmas gifts). *Gesundheit* doesn't really mean "bless you"; it means "health"—the good variety being implied. Psychiatrists speak of angst (fear) and practice Gestalt (form) psychology. When something is broken, it's kaput. Although not every English speaker knows that *Fahrvergnügen* is "driving pleasure," most do know that *Volkswagen* means "people's car." Musical works can have a leitmotiv. Our cultural view of the world is called a weltanschauung by historians or philosophers. Similar Germanic terms are commonly understood by most well-read English speakers.

Other words that are borrowed from German include blitz, cobalt, dachshund, delicatessen, ersatz, frankfurter, glockenspiel, hinterland, infobahn (for "information highway"), kaffeeklatsch, pilsner, pretzel, quartz, rucksack, sauerkraut, schnapps, strudel, waltz, and wiener. And from Low German we find brake, dote, and tackle.

Such borrowing is usually a two-way street. The German language, particularly since World War II (which also gave us the blitzkrieg), has likewise taken over the use of many English words—and even some pseudo-English words of which English speakers have never heard.

Many English words have become such an integral part of German that their English origins have largely been forgotten. Even the German Language Association has thrown in the towel on "German" words such as *der Award, das Baby, babysitten* (to babysit), *der Babysitter, das Bodybuilding, das Callgirl, der Camp, der Clown, der Cocktail, der Computer, fit* (in good shape), *die Garage, das Hobby, der Job, jobben* (work), *joggen* (to jog), *killen* (to kill), *der Killer, der Lift* (elevator), *managen* (to manage), *der Manager, das Musical, der Playboy, der Pullover, der Rum, der Smog, der Snob, der Streik* (strike), *das Team, der Teenager, das Ticket, der Trainer* (coach), and *der Tunnel*.

It may also be too late to protect German against the invasion of the possessive apostrophe, as in "Maria's Buch."

Pseudo-English Terms

The following are terms that many German speakers believe to be actual English words but that really exist only in German:

die Basecap = baseball cap

der Beamer = digital (LED) projector

der Dressman = male model

das Handy = cellular or mobile telephone

das Happy-End = happy ending in a movie

das Lifting = a face-lift or other plastic surgery

der Smoking = tuxedo, formal dinner jacket

der Talkmaster = talk show host

der Twen = someone in his or her 20s, as in "*Teens und Twens*"

German Abbreviations and Acronyms

Like English, German uses many acronyms and abbreviations that stand in for longer words. Since the German language has many long words, you need to know the more common shortened forms found in print, online, and in many aspects of daily life. Below you'll find a helpful list divided into several categories.

Pronunciation: This is a good reason to learn how to say the alphabet in German. VW in German is pronounced fow-vay. You *do* know how to spell out your name in German, right?

1. Daily Life

ADAC Allgemeiner Deutscher Automobil-Club, auto club like AAA in the United States

AfD Alternative für Deutschland, Alterna-tive for Germany, a right-wing, anti-immigrant political party, originally founded in 2013 as a euroskeptic party

ARD Arbeitsgemeinschaft der öffentlich-rechtlichen Rundfunkanstalten Deutschlands = the first channel (*das Erste*) public TV broadcaster and the public radio service in Germany (also see ZDF below)

BH (bay-hah) *Büstenhalter*, bra, brassiere

BKA Bundeskriminalamt, the German FBI

CDU Christliche Demokratische Union, Christian Democratic Union (Angela Merkel's political party; center right)

CSU Christlich-Soziale Union, the CDU's sister party in Bavaria

EU (eh-ooh) Europäische Union, European Union

FDP Freie Demokratische Partei, Free Democratic Party (liberal, pro-business)

Hbf Hauptbahnhof, the central/main train station

ICE (ee-say-eh) InterCityExpress, high-speed train

MEZ Mitteleuropäische Zeit, Central European Time (CET)

SPD Sozialdemokratische Partei Deutschlands, Social Democratic Party of Germany

TÜV (tyoof) Technische Überwachungs-verein, the German product-safety testing agency, most commonly encountered with vehicle registration

ZDF Zweites Deutsches Fernsehen, the second public TV channel

2. Business and Technology

AG Aktiengesellschaft—a corporation with shares freely traded on a German, Austrian or Swiss stock exchange (*Börse*)

DAX, Dax (dox) Deutscher Aktien-Index—a German stock index similar to the Dow-Jones Index in the United States

DB (day-bay) Deutsche Bahn, the main German railway company; when referring to the railway, it's *die Bahn* or *mit der Bahn* (by rail) in German.

e.V. eingeschriebener Verein, a registered association, usually a nonprofit

GmbH Gesellschaft mit beschränkter Haftung—limited, incorporated

KG Kommanditgesellschaft, a limited partnership

oHG offene Handelsgesellschaft, a general partnership

3. In Print (Magazines, Newspapers, Online)

Abb. Abbildung, illustration

d.h. *das heißt* = i.e. (that is)

dpa (day-pay-ah) Deutsche Presse-Agentur, German Press Agency

Lkw *Lastkraftwagen*, truck, lorry

Pkw *Personenkraftwagen*, automobile, passenger vehicle

u.a. *und andere(s)*, and others, among other things

usw. *und so weiter*, etc. (etcetera, and so on)

z.B. *zum Beispiel*, e.g. (for example)

German Radio and TV: Public Versus Private

Since a 1986 court opinion, Germany has had a dual broadcasting system, similar to Great Britain's, in which both private and public broadcasters have access to the airways, communications satellites, and cable transmissions. Germany's public broadcasting corporations (ARD and ZDF) are subject to supervision by three regulatory bodies: the Radio/Television Council (Rundfunk/Fernsehrat), the Administrative Council (Verwaltungsrat), and the Director General. The Radio/Television Council members are either elected by the 16-state (*Land*) parliaments or chosen by the political parties. The representatives must come from a variety of political, religious, and social groups. The council, which is to remain free of governmental influences, advises the Director General on programming issues. The Administration Council determines the budget and supervises the management.

As fair as the German system may sound in theory, German broadcasting is subject to the same political influences and biases that exist in any other country. When they were in power, Chancellor Kohl and his CDU party often objected to what they termed "bias in the media"—a phrase that also sounds familiar to Americans. Kohl's government, unhappy with German television coverage, at one time even threatened to change the broadcast laws. Notwithstanding, Germany's public and private broadcasters remain at least as unfettered as those in most other free, democratic countries. Despite some recent censorship moves, particularly regarding the Internet, Germany still ranks high in its degree of media freedom.

To finance its public broadcasting services, Germany (like Austria and Switzerland) imposes a fee called the *Rundfunkbeitrag* ("radio/TV contribution"), which in reality is a radio/TV-service tax that goes to ARD, DW, ZDF, etc. Prior to 2013, this "fee" was known as the GEZ (for the *Gebühreneinzugszentrale* agency that collected it). The new fee also reflects a major change in the law. Whereas the GEZ was ostensibly paid only by people with a radio and/or TV set, the new fee is per household, whether or not they have a radio or TV. In the age of broadband Internet and streaming, it has become impossible to distinguish between traditional and online broadcasting. Although the new fee per household is very unpopular, it has drastically cut down on *Schwarzfernsehen*, watching TV without paying for it.

Related Web links: German radio and TV channels (G): **ard.de**—ARD radio and television; **zdf.de**—ZDF television; **rbb.de**—RBB (Rundfunk Berlin–Brandenburg); **rtl.de**—RTL (commercial TV); **dw.com**—Deutsche Welle (in 30 languages); **rundfunkbeitrag.de**—Beitragsservice website; **arte.tv**—ARTE, French-German TV channel for the arts; **tagesschau.de**—ARD news broadcast

FSK—Film Ratings and Culture

Film censorship is as old as the film industry. So, while Germany has a long history of film censorship and film ratings, so do most other countries. Unlike the United Kingdom's BBFC, the Motion Picture Association of America claims that its ratings are merely guidelines, not censorship. Regardless, any movie rating system ends up being a kind of censorship, even if it claims otherwise, and the German rating system is no different.

In Germany, movie censorship began in Berlin in 1906 when the chief of police announced that all films would be subject to *Präventivzensur*, meaning they had to be screened and approved in advance of any public showing. In 1920, the German government passed the *Reichslichtspielgesetz*, or Imperial Motion Picture Law, that called for the approval (*Freigabe*) of any film to be exhibited anywhere in the Reich. During the Nazi era, strict control of the film industry and film distribution meant that any motion picture shown in Germany had a government seal of approval. Since 1949, all movies shown in Germany have been rated by the FSK (Freiwillige Selbstkontrolle der Filmwirtschaft). Despite its name, the FSK "Voluntary Self-Regulation of the Film Industry" is not at all voluntary. No film or video made in Hollywood, Germany, or anywhere else can be distributed in Germany without an FSK rating.

A country's film-rating system can reveal a lot about its culture. The first thing you notice in a comparison of Anglo-American versus German film ratings is the different emphasis placed on two important criteria: sex and violence. In contrast to the

U.S. system, the FSK approves films with "mild sexual situations" for ages 12 and above (*freigegeben ab 12 Jahren*). But a film with violent scenes usually can't be viewed by anyone under 16.

Germany's film-rating system skirts the German constitution's unambiguous statement that "no censorship shall take place" partly by falling under the country's *Jungendschutzgesetze*, its youth-protection laws.

FSK RATINGS

- *ohne Altersbeschränkung*—all ages admitted
- *ab 6*—age 6 and up
- *ab 12*—age 12 and up
- *ab 16*—age 16 and up
- *ab 18*—age 18 and up
- *Indiziert*—"indexed" films (mostly gory horror and violent porn), which are for adults only and can't be advertised or sold by mail; for DVD and video

Films can be banned entirely. Some 180 films are currently banned in Germany, which means they can't be sold or shown.

Related Web links: fsk.de—official site of the German film-ratings board (G); **bbfc.co.uk**—British Board of Film Classification (E); **mpaa.org**—Motion Picture Association of America (E)

The German Press

Even in the age of the Internet, television, smartphones, and online media, Germans continue their love affair with newspapers and magazines. Germany has a great variety of print publications on almost any topic. It is a media diversity found in few other countries.

But, following a worldwide trend, the circulation figures for periodicals in Germany has steadily declined over the past two decades. With few exceptions, most German newspapers and magazines have seen their circulation drop by about half since the late 1990s. Germany's newspaper circulation per 1,000 population dropped from 417 in 1995 to 255 in 2012. That still leaves Germany ahead of Britain (249 per 1,000), Canada (211), France (179), and the United States (166).

Article 5 of the German *Grundgesetz* (Basic Law, the German constitution) guarantees freedom of the press and the right of access to information. The watchdog group Freedom House gave Germany, Austria, and the United Kingdom each a press and democratic freedom score of 94 percent in 2017, higher than the United States (86 percent). Switzerland scored 96 percent and Canada 99 percent. Freedom House designates 88 countries as "free," representing 45 percent of the world's nations and 39 percent of the global population.

German newspapers and periodicals range from the so-called *Boulevardpresse* (tabloid press), led by the notorious, sensationalist daily *Bild* with its 1.7 million readers, to the highly respected weekly *Die Zeit* with under half a million readers. German and European attitudes about nudity mean that you are much more likely to see photos or ads with bare-breasted women in mainstream German publications than in comparable U.S. publications.

The *Frankfurter Allgemeine Zeitung* (FAZ) is Germany's *New York Times.* Munich-based *Focus* and Hamburg-based *Der Spiegel* are Germany's leading news weeklies, similar to *Time* and *Newseeek* in the United States. Most German print publications offer online or app subscriptions.

Major German Newspapers and Magazines (average circulation including e-editions, 2017)

DAILY NEWPAPERS (*TAGESZEITUNGEN*)
Berliner Zeitung 99,591
Bild-Zeitung (nationwide) 1,722,088
Frankfurter Allgemeine (FAZ, plus Sunday) 535,031
Süddeutsche Zeitung (Munich) 367,235
Die Zeit (Hamburg, weekly) 543,078

MAGAZINES (*ZEITSCHRIFTEN*)
Das Beste (*Reader's Digest*, monthly) 272,113
Bunte (Hamburg, illustrated weekly) 447,873
Focus (Munich, news weekly) 447,873
Der Spiegel (Hamburg, news weekly) 739,213
Stern (Hamburg, illustrated weekly) 547,480

Related Web links: German newspapers (G): bild.de—Bildzeitung; faz.net—Frankfurter Allgemeine, welt.de—Die Welt, zeit.de—Die Zeit German magazines (G): bunte.de—Bunte; focus .de—Focus; spiegel.de—Der Spiegel; stern.de—Stern; sueddeutsche.de—Süddeutsche Zeitung

From the Bonn Republic to the Berlin Republic

The two cities of Bonn and Berlin could hardly be more different: sleepy Bonn on the banks of the Rhine, bustling Berlin on the banks of the Spree. During the Cold War, from 1949 until after the fall of the Berlin Wall, Bonn (pop. 318,000) was the de facto capital of West Germany. Although Berlin (pop. 3.4 million) is now the capital (*Bundeshauptstadt*) and seat of government of the unified Federal Republic of Germany, many government ministries are still located in the "Federal City" (*Bundesstadt*) of Bonn. Officials regularly take the 50-minute flight between Bonn and Berlin, a distance of 480 km (298 mi) as the crow flies. (Driving, even on the autobahn, requires about 6 hours.) Critics point out the waste in time and money of having two centers of government. The estimated 20,000 work flights annually between the two cities costs 7.5 million euros and has considerable environmental impact. About one third of federal civil servants still work in Bonn.

Most non-Germans fail to grasp the deep divisions that the Bonn–Berlin debate caused in 1991. After more than five decades, West Germans had grown accustomed to having their capital in the quiet university town of Bonn, far removed from Berlin and its dark legacy of German nationalism run amok. Moving the capital back to Berlin meant a face-to-face confrontation with the city's—and the country's—Nazi past.

Berlin had already become the official federal capital as part of the German Unification Treaty signed in 1990, but the Bundestag still needed to vote to move the seat of government, or not. On June 20, 1991, after more than 10 hours of vigorous debate in Bonn, the legislators voted 338 to 320 to move the government to Berlin. The so-called Bonn/Berlin Law, passed by a narrow 18-vote margin, started the process of moving the German government and its institutions from Bonn to Berlin. Finally taking effect in 1994, the law also set in motion a massive construction project to complete the new and renovated structures to house those institutions. The highlight of this gradual process came on April 19, 1999, when the Bundestag held its first session in the Reichstag building in Berlin, with its new, gleaming metal-and-glass dome designed by British architect Norman Foster.

So why does Germany still have federal government offices in both Berlin and Bonn? To compensate Bonn for the bitter pill of losing the capital, the city got some sweeteners in the form of jobs in some government ministries and agencies. But Berlin is acting like a magnet, slowly pulling more and more agencies away from Bonn. However, politics will protect the Federal City for a while longer.

Related Web links: bundesregierung.de/Webs/Breg/EN/Homepage/_node.html—German Federal Government official site (E)

Berlin's Straße des 17. Juni cuts through the Tiergarten park to the Brandenburg Gate.

From Reichswehr to *Bundeswehr*: The German Armed Forces

Germany's *Bundeswehr* (federal defense force) consists of the army (*Bundesheer*), air force (*Luftwaffe*), and navy (*Bundesmarine*). Because of the Nazi era and tainted past of the military after World War II, Germany and the Allies wanted to avoid associations with the former Reichswehr and Hitler's Wehrmacht. Consequently, members of the military are considered "citizens in uniform" and are guaranteed constitutional rights.

In 1956, Germany imposed mandatory military service for all males over 18. The required term of service has varied from 15 months to the current 10 months (since 1996). Conscientious objectors (*Kriegsverweigerer*) can meet the draft requirement by doing public service in public institutions, but they must serve three months longer than those in military service.

Until recently, women in the military were limited to service in noncombat areas: medical and music. Germany's Basic Law constitution explicitly prevented women from bearing arms, but in October 2000, the Bundestag revised Article 12a to read that women could not be "compelled" to bear arms, thus allowing women to voluntarily do so. On July 2, 2001, for the first time in German history, 677 women began military service along with men in the armed forces.

After World War II, there were two German armed forces, one in the East and one in the West. The Nationale Volksarmee (NVA) of the German Democratic Republic was disbanded after German reunification in 1990 and merged with the western *Bundeswehr*.

Germany has been a member of NATO (North Atlantic Treaty Organization) since 1955, the same year that East Germany's NVA became part of the Soviet-led Warsaw Pact, and Germany's armed forces still constitute the largest single contingent of NATO troops in Europe. Allied/NATO troops from six nations were stationed in Germany, but in the years following reunification and the end of the Cold War, the U.S., British, French, and other troops have largely been withdrawn. In the 1990s, reunified Germany had to face its new military role as the European Union's largest and most influential country. Already in the 1980s, Germany had begun to debate the Basic Law's limitations on where and how German troops could serve. The Helmut Kohl government, reacting to outside criticism that Germany was not pulling its weight militarily, had slowly increased German participation in NATO operations, including the Persian Gulf War in 1991. It was not until 1994, though, that Germany's highest court ruled that German forces could participate in United Nations and joint UN-NATO peacekeeping missions with Bundestag approval. As a result, German troops were stationed in Kosovo in 1999 and in Afghanistan in 2002.

Related Web links: heer.bundeswehr.de—*Bundeswehr, Heer* (army) (E, G); **luftwaffe.de**—*Luftwaffe* (air force) (G); **deutschemarine.de**—*Bundesmarine* (navy) (G); **bundeswehr.de**—for information on all three services

The Rise of the Far Right in 21st-Century Germany

Germany's November 2017 federal election put a nationalist, right-wing, neo-Nazi party into the Bundestag, the national parliament, for the first time since West Germany's first post-war election in 1949. But the *Alternative für Deutschland* (AfD) party did not even exist before 2013, when it tried and failed to win seats in a national election.

Members of the Bundestag were going through political culture shock after 92 new AfD members took their seats following the 2017 election. (Out of the 94 AfD MPs elected, 2 left the party soon after the election.) The closest the Bundestag has ever come to having to deal with a far-right faction since World War II was when the *Deutsche Rechtspartei* (German Right Party) won five seats in the 1949 federal election. That national conservative right-wing party attracted former Nazis, but lost its seats in the next election.

There have been other German nationalist, rightist, neo-Nazi parties since then, but they were never able to win at the national level. The most notorious of these, the National Democratic Party of Germany (NPD), previously won scattered representation in some state parliaments, but never in the Bundestag.

The Alternative for Germany party was founded as an anti-euro-currency, anti-immigrant party similar to Britain's UKIP. After failing to clear the 5-percent hurdle for parliamentary representation in 2013, the AfD cleverly took advantage of growing anti-Muslim attitudes in Germany caused by a massive influx of refugees from war-torn regions in the Middle East. They played on several incidents of turmoil blamed on "foreigners" and also demonized chancellor Angela Merkel and her CDU/CSU party for welcoming the refugees. In the 2017 election, the AfD became Germany's third largest national party, gaining 12.6 percent of the vote. AfD support was strongest in the east and south. In the eastern state of Saxony (*Sachsen*) the AfD even won a majority.

On February 22, 2018, during an emotional speech to the full Bundestag, former Green Party leader Cem Özdemir vigorously lashed out at the AfD, accusing its members of seeking to impose Nazi-style press censorship and "despising everything modern Germany stands for." Responding to an earlier AfD political rally at which the crowd called for him to be deported from Germany because of his Turkish roots, Mr. Özdemir, who was born in Germany to immigrant parents, said "It's easier than they think," adding that he would soon return to his Swabian hometown in southwestern Germany. "That's my home and I will not let you break it. This Germany is stronger than your hate will ever be." His stirring words rapidly spread across Germany in a viral video and in media reports.

Related Web links: **bundestag.de**—official Bundestag website (G, E); **dw.de**—Deutsche Welle for German cultural/political news (E, other languages)

Political Parties in Germany

Germany has over 15 active main parties, plus at least as many minor parties that have limited influence and few members. Each of Germany's traditional political parties has three main things: (1) a core political philosophy, (2) an abbreviation or nickname, and (3) an identifying color. The principal national political parties are described below.

Christian Democratic Union (CDU) / Christian Social Union (CSU)

Color: Black. Founded: 1950

The conservative CDU and its Bavarian CSU sister party have played a significant role in modern German history, governing for a total of 47 years up to 2017. Founding father Konrad Adenauer led the party as chancellor from 1949 to 1963. Since 2005, Angela Merkel has headed the CDU/CSU and held the office of chancellor over four terms.

Social Democratic Party (SPD)

Color: Red. Founded: 1875 (Germany's oldest political party)

Traditionally the party of the working classes and labor unions, the SPD is strongest in industrial regions. In recent years, it has partnered with the CDU/CSU, but the SPD won only about 20 percent of the vote in 2017.

Free Democratic Party (FDP)

Color: Yellow. Founded: 1948

The pro-business, neo-liberal FDP has long been a permanent fixture in the German Bundestag, but the party suffered major losses in 2013, failing to clear the 5-percent hurdle to enter parliament. But it made a comeback in the 2017 elections, gaining a 10.7 percent share of the vote. Though it has never led a German government, the FDP has played kingmaker to both the CDU and the SPD over the years.

The Green Party (*Bündnis 90/Die Grünen*, "The Greens")

Color: Green. Founded: 1980s, out of several counterculture parties

As its name implies, the Greens (Alliance/The Greens) emphasize environmental and social issues. Its members tend to be well-educated, urban, affluent voters. Originally made up of young rebels, today fewer than 10 percent of Green voters are under 35. The Greens won just under 9 percent of the 2017 vote.

Alternative for Germany (AfD)

Color: Light blue. Founded: 2013, originally as a euroskeptic party

The right-wing, nationalist *Alternative für Deutschland* (AfD) has surged to prominence by appealing to Germans who oppose the recent flood of refugees from war-torn Muslim countries. The AfD is now in every state parliament as well as the European parliament.

The Left party (*Die Linke*)

Color: Red (magenta in media coverage to distinguish it from the SPD)

Founded in 2007, The Left is an outgrowth of the East German Socialist Unity Party (SED), and the PDS (1989–2007) following reunification. "Left" voters tend to be former communists who supported the German Democratic Republic (GDR) and protest voters expressing their disenchantment with traditional parties.

Related Web links: German parties (G): **spd.de**—Sozialistische Partei Deutschlands; **cdu.de**—Christliche Demokratische Union; **csu.de**—Christliche Sozialistische Union; **gruene.de**—Bündnis 90/Die Grüne; **liberale.de**—Frei Demokratische Partei (FDP)

General: **politik-digital.de**—German politics online (G)

The renovated Reichstag, with its new glass dome, draws tourists from all over the world.

Jamaica, Traffic-Light, and Other Colorful Coalitions

Political coalitions have a long history in Germany, going back to the Weimar Republic (1919–1933). More recently, in the Federal Republic of Germany since 1949, political coalitions have formed governments by having two or more parties work together to form a majority government in parliament (*der Bundestag*). This is also common practice in Germany's state legislatures.

Sometimes a coalition is a so-called grand coalition. This term goes back to the Weimar era, but in modern usage in Germany, a grand coalition is a partnership between the two political parties that won the most seats/votes, when it also would be numerically possible to form a coalition among several smaller parties. However, an alliance of smaller parties is not always politically desirable or possible. Enter the grand coalition, *die Große Koalition*. (The short form, *GroKo*, was the German word of year in 2013.)

In post–World War II Germany, the first grand coalition at the federal level was formed in 1966 by the SPD and the CDU/CSU, the two major political parties at that time. Following a dispute with the FDP over tax increases, a new government needed to be formed between the SPD and Kurt Georg Kiesinger's CDU. That grand coalition controlled 95 percent of the Bundestag and lasted until 1969. Germany's second and third grand coalitions were formed under Angela Merkel beginning in 2005.

In the 2017 federal election, at which time chancellor Angela Merkel was trying to form a government for her fourth term, when the votes were counted, her CDU/CSU party had won only 33 percent of the vote. After twice governing together with the CDU/CSU in a grand coalition (2005–2009 and 2013–2017), the Social Democrats (SPD), under Martin Schulz, declined to do so again. So work began on a "Jamaica coalition," named for the colors of Jamaica's flag and those of the parties involved: the CDU/CSU (black), the FDP (yellow), and the Greens. But after months passed, and it became obvious that a *Jamaika-Koalition* was not going to fly, Schulz and the SPD agreed to GroKo talks. A CDU-SPD coalition is also called *Schwarz-Rot* (Black-Red).

The 1998 German word of the year was *Rot-Grün* (Red-Green), a term derived from the colors of a coalition formed that year by the SPD (red) and The Greens (green). But an even more colorful coalition is the *Ampelkoalition*, the traffic-light coalition, named for an SPD-FDP-Greens alliance reflecting the red, yellow, and green colors of a traffic signal. Although there never has been one at the national level, traffic-light coalitions have governed in Brandenburg (1990–1994) and in Bremen (1991–1995).

Related Web link: en.wikipedia.org/wiki/List_of_ political_parties_in_Germany—Major and minor parties at federal and state level (E)

The Religious Split: From Pagan Unity to Christian Division

Around A.D. 350, the Visigoth bishop Ulfilas (Wulfila) completed the first translation of the Bible into *Gotisch*, an early form of German. By the second half of the eighth century, all of the pagan Germanic peoples had been Christianized. Today Germany's population is almost evenly split between Roman Catholics (*römisch-katholisch*) and Protestants (*evangelisch*). Although most of the Catholics live in Bavaria in southern Germany, and the Protestants in north Germany, there are pockets of Catholicism in the Rhineland northern cities such as Cologne (Köln), while the southwestern state of Baden-Württemberg is largely Protestant. Muslims, Jews, and people of other minority faiths make up less than 4 percent of Germany's population.

Germany was home to the Protestant Reformation, which began in Wittenberg in 1517 when Martin Luther expressed his objections to the church practice of selling indulgences, by tacking his "95 Theses" to the door of Wittenberg's All Saints church (as legend has it). The Reformation continued in Germany as well as Switzerland by Philipp Melanchthon (Augsburg), Huldrych Zwingli (Zurich), John Calvin (Geneva), and other reformers. By 1526, the Protestants were already split into the Reformed and Lutheran divisions. In 1530, Melanchthon drafted the Augsburg Confession (Augsburger Bekenntnis), the "constitution" of both the Lutheran faith and the Schmalkaldic League.

It is an irony of history that in eastern Germany, the location of *die Lutherstadt Wittenberg*, the city most identified with the Reformer, traditional religion virtually died out during the Communist years. The East German government was amazingly successful in stamping out the "opiate of the people" and replacing it with many secular practices including the secular *Jugendweihe* confirmation. However, East Germany's Lutheran churches nurtured the rebellion that led to the end of the GDR in 1990.

Religion is a compulsory subject in German secondary schools. Separate classes are taught for Protestants and Catholics (and in some cases for Jews and Muslims). For others there is an ethics course (*Ethik*). Students over the age of 14 can opt out of religious or ethical instruction.

Although today the influence of the Mormons, born-again Christians, and other "sects" as well as growing numbers of Islamic faithful can be seen, most German speakers, even those who consider themselves Protestant or Catholic, rarely set foot in a house of worship.

Protestant

The word *Protestant* comes from the second imperial Diet of Speyer in 1529. A minority opinion, a *protestation*, was issued on behalf of those princes who objected to the diet's reversal of a decision by the first Diet of Speyer in 1526 that rulers in the empire could each determine the religion of their own realms. In German, the word *evangelisch* is most often used for "Protestant"—less often *protestantisch*.

Related Web links: ekd.de—Vereinigte Evangelisch-Lutheranische Kirche Deutschlands (United Lutheran Church of Germany) (G); **dbk.de/katholische-kirche/**—Katholische Kirche (G)

Church and State

While Germany has no official state church, as with the Lutheran Church in Sweden, the German government collects "church tax" (*die Kirchensteuer*) from the country's Protestants, Catholics, and Jews (but not from Muslims). Through a unique state-church partnership, the government imposes a tax, via the income tax, to support church schools, churches, and other installations. Although the *Grundgesetz* (German constitution) guarantees religious freedom, this kind of close cooperation between government and church would be considered unconstitutional in the United States and many other countries. But the German brand of state-church cooperation goes beyond the *Kirchensteuer*. German clergy and priests are educated mostly in tax-supported public colleges and universities, and the churches have the right to choose the faculty members of departments of theology. For their part, the churches help staff and run schools, hospitals, homes for elderly people (*Altenheime*).

It's logical that in the homeland of Martin Luther, most of Germany's Protestants are Lutheran. Die *Evangelische Kirche in Deutschland* (EKD, the Protestant Church in Germany), headquartered in Hannover, is an association of 24 largely independent Lutheran churches, the largest being the Augsburg Confession (*Augsburger Bekenntnis*). The EKD and its members regard non-Lutheran Protestants, *die Freikirchen* (free churches)—Methodists, Mormons, Jehovah's Witnesses, and so forth—as *Sekten* (sects) and not "true" Protestant churches.

The East German Protestant church played a major role in bringing down the Communist German Democratic Republic. Protestant churches all across the GDR became centers for protests that eventually led to the 1989 collapse of East Germany and the fall of the Berlin Wall. Ironically, many eastern Germans have turned their backs on the church that helped win their freedom. The rate of church membership and attendance in the east is considerably lower than in the west.

Following German reunification, the Roman Catholic Church, *die katholische Kirche*, added only 4 East German dioceses (*Bistümer*) or archdioceses (*Erzbistümer*), for a total of 27, after its reorganization in 1994.

Germany's two major faiths get along well, without the serious tensions found in some other parts of the world, actively cooperating at the local, regional, and national levels as well as in international ecumenical organizations such as the World Council of Churches.

The *Kirchensteuer* is collected by the government for the Protestant, Roman Catholic, and Jewish denominations. The church tax amounts to approximately 8 to 9 percent of the income tax for the tax year. Some Germans avoid the church tax by officially leaving the church (not possible in all *Länder*). Foreign nationals are also exempt if they have no official registered religious affiliation. Because German taxpayers can deduct the *Kirchensteuer* from their taxable income, resulting in lost tax revenue, this church support amounts to a government subsidy.

The Bible in German: From Ulfilas to Luther

Essentially, every Bible is a translation (*eine Übersetzung*). The ancient elements that became what we now call the Bible (*die Bibel*) were originally written in Hebrew, Aramaic, and Greek on papyrus, leather, and clay. The earliest Germanic version of the Bible was Ulfilas's Gothic translation from Latin and Greek. From Ulfilas came much of the Germanic Christian vocabulary that is still in use today. Later, in the ninth century, Charlemagne (Karl der Große) fostered Frankish (Germanic) translations. Over the years, prior to the appearance of the first printed German Bible in 1466, various German and German dialect translations of the Scriptures were published. The *Augsburger Bibel* of 1350 was a complete New Testament; the Wenzel Bible (1389) contained the Old Testament in German.

Johannes Gutenberg's famous 42-line Bible, printed in Mainz, was in Latin. About 40 copies exist today in various states of completeness. It was Gutenberg's invention of printing from movable type that made the Bible, in any language, vastly more influential and important by making possible the production of books in greater quantities at a lower cost.

In 1466, before Martin Luther was even born, a German Bible that was a literal translation of the Latin Vulgate was published using Gutenberg's invention of movable type. Known as the Mentel Bible, it was printed in Strasbourg and appeared in some 18 editions until it was replaced by Luther's new translation in 1522.

The most influential German Bible, and the one that continues to be most widely used in the Germanic world (last official revised edition in 1984), was translated from the original Hebrew and Greek by Martin Luther (1483–1546) in the record time of just 10 weeks (New Testament), during his involuntary stay in the Wartburg Castle in Wittenberg. Luther's first complete Bible in German appeared in 1534. He continued to revise his translations up until his death. In response to Luther's Protestant Bible, the German Catholic Church published its own versions, most notably the *Emser Bibel*, which became the standard German Catholic Bible. Luther's German Bible also became the primary source for other northern European versions in Danish, Dutch, and Swedish.

In 1524, having been barred by church authorities from creating a new English version of the Bible in England, the English scholar and translator William Tyndale went to Germany. Financed by London merchants, Tyndale's translation of the New Testament was published in Cologne in 1525, and later in Worms. Copies of his new translation reached England in 1526, but Tyndale paid a high price for his efforts. Before he could complete his work on the Old Testament, he was captured in Belgium and later burned at the stake (1536) for his "untrue translations." His Bibles were burned, but his work proved to be a lasting influence on English Bible translation in later centuries, including the venerable King James Version of 1611.

Muslims in Germany

When the Turkish grand vizier, Kara Mustafa, tried to take Vienna in 1683, among the forces that defeated the Ottoman Turks were troops from Bavaria, Franconia, Saxony, and Swabia—all now states or regions of Germany. That famous battle on the Kahlenberg Hills had two major results: the end of the Turkish invasions of Europe and the start of Austrian and German coffeehouses.

So, there is some irony in the fact that Muslim Turks today are the largest ethnic minority living in Germany. The first generation of immigrant Turks came to Germany in the early 1960s as *Gastarbeiter* (guest workers) to "temporarily" fill a labor shortage in Germany's booming postwar economy during the *Wirtschaftswunder* (economic miracle). But few of them ever returned home, and soon their children were growing up, speaking German, and having families of their own.

The country's Islamic population is now approaching 5 million and growing, although not all are devout, religious Muslims. Over 60 percent of Muslims in Germany are of Turkish origin. A 2017 Pew Research Center report predicted that Muslims could make up 9 to 20 percent of the German population by 2050. Muslims in Germany are younger and have a higher birth rate than the non-Muslim population. Even if immigration were to stop, the Muslim population would still grow. For historical reasons, there are very few Muslims in eastern Germany, but there are mosques in Chemnitz and Leipzig.

The oldest existing mosque (*Moschee*) in Germany was built in Berlin's Wilmersdorf district between 1924 and 1928. The *Berliner Moschee*, or *Ahmadiyya-Moschee*, is still in use today. It is now one of five mosques in Berlin, the latest (Ibn Rushd-Goethe, 2017) being a so-called liberal mosque, which allows men and women to worship together and bans burqas and face veils.

Almost every larger German city, from Hamburg to Munich, has one or more mosques. Cologne's Central Mosque, the largest in Germany, with two 55-meter tall minarets, opened in 2017 following many years of controversy and delays. The German newspaper *Die Zeit* estimated that there are about 2,750 mosques in Germany, compared to about 45,000 Christian churches (2016).

Germany's first Muslim cemetery was established in Berlin in 1798, when the Turkish ambassador to Prussia, Ali Aziz Efendi, was laid to rest there. In 1866, the cemetery moved to its current location at the mosque in Neukölln. When it ran out of room (Islam does not allow graves to be "recycled," as is the German custom), a new Islamic section was opened in the *Landschaftsfriedhof Gatow* in 2012. Increasing numbers of Muslims in Germany want to be buried in Germany, which means that Islamic burial customs must be accommodated, including that the grave must be pointed toward Mecca.

Related Web link: zentralmoschee-koeln.de—Central Mosque, Cologne (G)

German Jews

In the years just prior to World War II, Germany was home to about 530,000 Jews. Today, out of a total population of 81 million, only about 61,000 Germans are members of Jewish congregations in Germany, along with 10,000 estimated nonmembers. Since the registered Jewish population was only about 28,000 in 1990, most of those in Germany today are recent Eastern European and Russian Jewish arrivals. With the country's having such a low Jewish population, few Germans have ever known a Jew personally. Despite this fact, the issue of Jews and their history in Germany continues to dominate many aspects of the German religious, cultural, and political landscape. Jews and Jewish issues are featured much more prominently in the German media than the population numbers would indicate, especially when compared with Germany's largest religious minority, the 3.2 million Muslims (mostly Turks).

Germany's Jewish community is represented by the Central Council of Jews in Germany (Zentralrat der Juden in Deutschland), which has its headquarters in Bonn. The German Institute for Jewish Studies (die Hochschule für Jüdische Studien) was established in 1980 in Heidelberg. The *Zentralarchiv*, a large archive for research on the history of the Jews in Germany, was established in 1987, also in Heidelberg. Ignatz Bubis, the head of the *Zentralrat* from 1992 until his death in 1999, was often seen on television and in the news commenting on various issues.

It is in Berlin that today's Jewish presence is most apparent. Almost one in five of the country's Jews lives in the German capital.

The new, starkly appealing Jewish Museum by the Polish-American architect Daniel Libeskind became a popular destination even before its exhibits were completed. Berlin's stark Memorial to the Murdered Jews of Europe (*Denkmal für die Ermordeten Juden Europas*) on 4.7 acres just south of the Brandenburg Gate and the U.S. Embassy was designed by the American architect Peter Eisenman. A difficult-to-find underground information center/museum contains the names of about 3 million Jewish Holocaust victims. Built at a cost of 25 million euros, the memorial opened to the public in May 2005.

Berlin in the 1920s had a thriving community of liberal Reform Jews who were trying to change from the traditional Orthodox ways (more participation by women, organs in synagogues, and so forth). That all ended with the Nazis and the war, and today most of Germany's Jews (few of them born in Germany) are either Orthodox or nonpracticing. On the bright side, Berlin has again become the center of progressive or Reform Judaism in Germany. However, the Jewish factions are facing the issue of tax support, since only Orthodox Judaism is considered Germany's official Jewish group and thus receives all church-tax funding.

Related Web links: jmberlin.de—Jewish Museum in Berlin (E, G); **berlin-judentum.de**—Jewish Berlin (E, G)

Germany and Scientology: Persecution or Objectivity?

The word *sect* (*die Sekte*) in German carries much the same negative tone as *cult* in English (also *der Kult* in German) but with added implications of illegality and fraud. *Eine Sekte* is just about any Christian religious group that is not a part of the two mainstream German churches, the Catholics and the Lutherans. Although the word applies to Baptists, Methodists, Mormons, Presbyterians, and other "sects" in Germany and other German-speaking countries, it is more often used to refer to Jehovah's Witnesses (*die Zeugen Jehovas*) and, particularly, the Church of Scientology in Germany.

While Germans tend to look askance at any "sect," the Church of Scientology has been targeted for attacks by German church leaders, lawmakers, and private citizens. Ever since the American founder of Scientology, L. Ronald Hubbard, opened the first offices in Hamburg back in 1970, Scientology has been a lightning rod.

Books accusing the Church of Scientology of everything from being a danger to the German economy to "psychological terrorism" and the use of kidnapping and extortion have often been on German best-seller lists. There are several German anti-Scientology websites, at least one of them an "official" site run by the state of Nordrhein-Westfalen. State and federal government agencies have implemented bans against Scientologists. In 1996, the state of Bavaria barred anyone connected with Scientology from holding government jobs. Berlin requires contractors for state work to declare that they have no ties to Scientology. Even the U.S. delivery service UPS has been accused by a German consumer group of financially supporting the Church of Scientology. One might think that there are millions of Scientologists in Germany, while in fact estimates range from a mere 30,000 to 70,000.

Not that Scientology is without its critics in other places, but the degree of persecution and prosecution in Germany has led to accusations of Nazi-like religious intolerance, especially after anti-Scientology boycotts in 1996 against the film *Mission Impossible* and actor Tom Cruise. (The movie was still a big hit in Germany.) Such moves led to an unsuccessful series of newspaper ads in the *International Herald Tribune* and the *New York Times* (no German papers would carry the ads) that attempted to cast Germany's persecution of Scientology in the same light as German anti-Jewish attacks of the 1930s. In a country where it is illegal to display the Nazi swastika or to sell a copy of *Mein Kampf*, such comparisons only served to increase the level of anti-Scientology sentiment.

Related Web links: **verfassungsschutz.de**—Bundesamt für Verfassungsschutz a government "constitutional protection" site that has an anti-Scientology section (G); **scientology.org**—Church of Scientology (E)

Aspirin® or aspirin? A Classic Medicine and a Lost Trademark

Aspirin (*das Aspirin*) marked its 100th birthday in 1997. Although some two thousand years ago, the Greek Hippocrates knew of the painkilling properties of aspirin's main natural ingredient, which is extracted from the bark of willow trees, it was a German chemist who invented what we now know as aspirin, on August 10, 1897. Dr. Felix Hoffmann, in the employ of Bayer AG's predecessor Farbenfabriken vormals Friedr. Bayer & Co, was attempting to find an improved pain reliever for his father's arthritis when he discovered acetylsalicylic acid (ASA; *Azetylsalizylsäure*, or ASS, in German). The new compound was named "aspirin" as a result of combining the *a* in *Azetyl-*, *spir* from the Latin/Greek-based *Spirsäure* (salicylic acid, for the plant genus *Spiraea*, in which this natural acid is found), and the Latin *in*, for "found in." But Bayer (BYE-er) didn't register its new drug with the Imperial Patent Office in Berlin, or market it, until 1899.

Neither Hippocrates nor Hoffmann knew how aspirin's key ingredient performs its magic. Another 74 years went by before ASA's secrets were revealed by British researcher John Vane in 1971. (For his discovery, Vane received the 1982 Nobel Prize in medicine.) And more than a century after Felix Hoffmann's synthesis of acetylsalicylic acid, this longtime staple of medicine cabinets around the globe continues to amaze. The more that modern science reveals about aspirin, the more miraculous it seems. Since the 1960s, it has been used in the treatment of thrombosis and other blood-clotting ailments. More recently, aspirin has gained new respect for its preventive effects against strokes, heart attacks, and possibly even some cancers.

This does not mean that the wonder analgesic is for everyone. Some people are allergic to aspirin, and it has been linked to gastrointestinal irritation and the more serious Reye's syndrome. Yet, despite more recent competitors such as acetaminophen and ibuprofen, aspirin can still claim benefits that other drugs can't, particularly for certain heart conditions.

Although Bayer's old invention is still a valid registered trademark in at least 70 countries, in the United States and many other nations, *aspirin* long ago became a generic term, and Bayer lost its legal claim to the word that the company had coined.

These days, Bayer's aspirin plant in Bitterfeld churns out about a third of the world's total 50,000 tons of aspirin each year. Nevertheless, you can't buy a bottle of aspirin over the counter in Germany. As explained in the "Health and Fitness" chapter, in the land of its invention (and in Austria and Switzerland), aspirin is available only in an *Apotheke* (pharmacy, chemist's shop). And you'll need to ask for it by its trademarked name, Aspirin.

Related Web links: bayer.de—Bayer AG (E, G); bayeraspirin.com—Bayer, Inc. (E)

Germans in Space: *Deutsche im Weltall*

You may know that the German astronaut (*Raumfahrer*) Alexander Gerst spent 165 days aboard the 2014 International Space Station (ISS) expedition 40/41, along with an American. But do you know who the first German in space was? Well, neither do most Germans. It happened in 1978, and you'll find the answer below.

Neither the Russian nor the American space programs would have gotten off the ground as rapidly as they did without the talents and experience of the rocket scientists they imported from occupied Germany at the end of World War II. So it seems only fair that the Russians and Americans have invited Germans (and the Swiss Claude Nicolier) to participate in their space missions over the years.

So far, 11 German astronauts and cosmonauts have ventured into space on American or Russian rockets for various NASA, ESA, and ISS missions. The first was cosmonaut Sigmund Jähn, a citizen of the German Democratic Republic. The East German air force officer became the first German in orbit on August 26, 1978, on board the Soviet *Soyuz 31* spacecraft. Along with his Russian commander, Jähn linked up with and boarded the *Salyut 6* space station (*Raumstation*), where he performed scientific experiments during an 8-day flight orbiting the earth 125 times. An exhibit honoring the "Hero of the GDR" and his space mission is located in Jähn's hometown of Morgenröthe-Rautenkranz.

In 1983, the first West German astronaut, Ulf Merbold, made two trips aboard the U.S. space shuttle *Columbia*. Ten years later, in 1993, two German astronauts were the first from reunited Germany to orbit the earth. Hans Schlegel and Ulrich Walter were the sixth and seventh Germans in orbit when they went into space for the D2 Spacelab mission with five American astronauts. Walter later led the development of the satellite imaging database for Germany's DLR space agency.

The backup payload specialist on the ground at the DLR Control Center in Germany for the 1993 D2 mission was physicist Gerhard Thiele. After training with NASA in Texas, Thiele completed his only spaceflight, the STS-99 Shuttle Radar Topography Mission in February 2000. Aboard the space shuttle *Endeavour*, Thiele used German X-SAR radar technology for a 3-D mapping project.

Decades earlier, the German-American Wernher von Braun (1912–1977) served as the first director of NASA's Marshall Space Flight Center from 1960 to 1970. Von Braun became a U.S. citizen in 1955, just 2 years before the *Jupiter C* rocket he had developed launched the first U.S. satellite (*Explorer 1*) into earth orbit. The historic 1969 Apollo 11 moon landing was largely made possible by the German V-2 rocket background of von Braun and the giant Saturn V rocket that he and his team at NASA developed.

Related Web links: dlr.de—German Aerospace Center (E, G); dlr.de/dlr/en/desktopdefault.aspx/tabid-10366/—biographical data on German astronauts (E)

Das Handy ... and Then Came the iPhone

The German word for mobile or cell phone, *das Handy*, is unfamiliar to most English speakers, but almost every German today uses a *Handy*. The roots of the German term may go back to a designation used by Motorola in the early days of mobile communication: the Handie-Talkie SCR536 AM portable two-way radio (1940).

Digital wireless phone service was introduced earlier and more widely in Europe than in North America. European mobile phone carriers offered features and services such as SMS text messaging and Web access before they were available in North America. But then an American technical revolution changed everything.

Apple's iPhone was released on June 29, 2007, and the world has never been the same since. Steve Jobs had envisioned a product like the iPhone back in the early 2000s, but it required many technological advances and a lot of visionary thinking to finally produce a true "smartphone" that combined the features of a tablet screen and a cell phone. The iPhone has evolved to a point where we now take this amazing miniature TV screen–telephone–computer combination for granted.

Partly due to the iPhone and its many imitators, the problems caused by the differences between North America's CDMA and Europe's GSM cell phone technology have largely vanished. Most smartphones today can function effortlessly almost anywhere in the world, so-called world phones. When the iPhone first came on the market, AT&T was the exclusive provider in the United States, while in Germany T-Mobile (now Telekom) had that role. While the iPhone is no longer exclusive, AT&T and T-Mobile USA are the only two U.S. cell phone carriers that use GSM technology (plus Bell and Rogers in Canada). But most phones with a SIM card will work in Europe. The SIM card (now more like a small chip) is a GSM feature that allows a mobile phone to easily be used with different providers, even in different countries.

Roaming in the European Union

As of 2017, the European Union has made it cheaper to use your mobile phone when traveling from Germany to France or from Germany to Austria, for instance. This makes EU roaming much more, although not entirely, like U.S. roaming. There are time limits on how long you can use, say, your German-based smartphone in Italy. Check with your carrier.

For Americans traveling in Europe, currently T-Mobile USA offers the best international roaming rates (20 cents/min) for Europe, Mexico, and other regions. Note: If you need to buy a new iPhone for Europe, purchase it in the United States rather than Germany/Europe. You'll save a lot of money!

Related Web link: telekom.com—Deutsche Telekom, the main German telecom (G), motorolasolutions.com/en_us/about/company-overview/history/timeline.html—development of the Handy (G, E)

Telefonieren: The Telecom Landscape in Germany

Germany and most of Europe long ago deregulated the telecommunications market and eliminated the old state-run PTT (post/telephone/telegraph) monopoly known as *die gelbe Post* ("the yellow postal service").

Born in 1999, privatized Deutsche Telekom AG remains Germany's dominant telecom. Now magenta-colored, Telekom does have some competition from O₂, 1&1 Versatel, and Vodafone, but early competitors that helped drive phone rates down have gradually vanished through buyouts and mergers. Now defunct Arcor, for example, was the first German phone company to introduce flat-rate monthly fees (in 2004). Before that, figuring out the cost of a phone call was a nightmare of per-minute charges, six different time periods, and geographic zones. Although phone costs in Germany have dropped by at least 65 percent since 2004, Germans still pay a bit more than other Europeans for telephone and Internet service.

Today, under the name Telekom Deutschland GmbH, Telekom is still notorious for poor service and long waits for a new landline (*Festnetz*) or Internet connection. But switching to another provider can bring its own headaches. As in most of the world, you now have a somewhat bewildering choice of telephone options in Germany, even just for what used to be a basic landline: digital, analog, ISDN, DSL, cable, fiber optics, various broadband speeds, etc. Subscribers also have to be aware of low introductory phone-plus-Internet rates for the first 6 or 12 months that rise dramatically later in a 24-month contract.

Even German telephone numbers can be confusing. Unlike in the United States, German phone numbers have varying lengths. Prefixes (area codes, *Vorwahl*) can be two to five digits (after a zero). Berlin is 030, while nearby Oranienburg is 03301. Cologne is 0221. Munich is 089. Cell-phone prefixes are unique, depending on the provider and not the geographic location. When you see a number with a 0160, 0170, or 0171 prefix, you know it's a mobile number, not a landline. A 0800 prefix is a toll-free call, but that's rare in Germany. Usually you have to pay 14 euro cents per minute to call a company about a problem!

The dialing procedure for a German phone number depends on where you are. If you're calling a Berlin number from Berlin, you dial the number without the 030 area code. But if you're calling from Munich, you have to dial 030 and the number. If you're making a call from outside Germany, you have to dial 00 (or + on a cell phone), the country code for Germany (49) and the city code (30), but without the zero!

Finding a public pay phone or telephone booth (*Telefonzelle*) in Germany is increasingly difficult. From 110,000 pay phones in 2006, the number dropped to 70,000 by 2010. In 2016, there were just over 17,000 in all of Germany. You can still find them in Germany, Austria, and Switzerland, but mostly at airports, train stations, and in shopping zones. The rise of the mobile phone plus mounting vandalism costs has reduced the number of pay phones, the first of which appeared in Berlin in 1881.

Related Web links: **telekom.de**—Deutsche Telekom, Germany's traditional phone monopoly is now a public corporation facing increasing telecom competition on many fronts (E, G); **o2online.de**—O₂, the trading name of telefónica Europe (G); **Vodafone.de**—Vodafone, British telecommunication company (G)

Swisscom pay phone

The Internet in Germany

Comparing Internet and World Wide Web usage depends on how you measure it. Do you want to count social media engagement, broadband speeds and costs, or the percentage of the population with Internet access? About 88 percent of Germans have Internet access, which is not very different from the figures for Canada and the United States: 88.5 percent for both (in 2016). But many European countries have a higher rate of access. In Norway, 98 percent of the population has an Internet connection. However, in Germany, if you count only the German population under age 60, the rate jumps to about 96 percent.

A DSL phone-line connection is still the most common type of Internet access in Germany, but cable, satellite, mobile, and fiber optics are also options. Germany's average download speed in 2015 was 12.9 Mbps (megabits per second), but that same year Tele Columbus began offering cable broadband service with speeds of up to 400 Mbps. The German government once promised that every home in Germany would have a minimum Internet access speed of 50 Mbps by 2018, but so far that goal remains unfulfilled. In 2017, the average cost of a flat-rate broadband connection in Germany was about 30 euros per month, depending on the speed and type of connection. Germany ranked 24th worldwide in connection speed (18.8 Mbps), 44th in cost, while the United States was 21st in speed (20 Mbps), and 114th in cost. Germany is far behind in FTTH (Fiber To The Home, fiber optics) coverage, with less than 2 percent. FTTH coverage in most European countries ranges from 5 to 12 percent.

Internet connection speeds will vary widely by location, type of broadband connection, and how much you're willing to pay. By the time you read this, average connection speeds will probably be higher, as speeds have risen rapidly over the past few years. For instance, Switzerland's average speed climbed from 16.7 Mbps in 2015 to 21.7 Mbps in 2017.

See the two tables below for more global comparisons in cost and speed.

Average Broadband Speed (2017)

Rank	Country	Mbps
1	Singapore	55.13
2	Sweden	40.16
3	Taiwan	34.4
4	Denmark	33.54
5	Netherlands	33.52
10	**Switzerland**	26.93
12	Japan	24.47
16	South Korea	22.9
21	United States	20.0
24	**Germany**	18.8
26	Canada	18.03
31	United Kingdom	16.51
34	**Austria**	15.26
37	France	13.43

Average Monthly Broadband Cost (2017)

Rank	Country	USD
28	Mexico	$26.66
40	Taiwan	$27.52
44	**Germany**	$34.08
49	France	$36.36
57	Singapore	$38.75
62	United Kingdom	$40.44
67	Spain	$41.61
77	Netherlands	$47.71
81	**Austria**	$50.11
92	Canada	$54.90
97	Sweden	$56.15
104	Australia	$60.37
114	United States	$66.17
143	**Switzerland**	$81.29

Sources: businessinsider.com/graph-ranks-countries-by-their-internet-speed-2017-8; cable.co.uk/media-centre/release/new-worldwide-broadband-price-league-unveiled

Society and Social Strata: *die oberen Zehntausend* and the *Mittelstand*

Germany is a wealthy country, one of the most prosperous nations in Europe and the world. In 2016, its average per capita annual household disposable income ($33,652 USD) was the European Union's highest, ahead of Britain, France, and Italy. (Non-EU member Switzerland ranked higher.) The Office of Economic Cooperation and Development (OECD) per capita average was $30,563.

According to Oxfam, the world's richest 1 percent held 82 percent of the wealth created in 2017. That came to $762 billion (€620 billion), which would be enough to end poverty seven times over. Germany is no exception in the disparity between rich and poor. Germany's crème de la crème elite, known as *die oberen Zehntausend* ("the upper 10,000") in German, hold an oversized proportion of the nation's wealth. In 2017, Germany ranked third in the number of billionaires, behind only China and the United States at the top. (See "Germany and the World Billionaires Count.")

Germany is also home to about 1.2 million U.S. dollar millionaires. Most of these moderately wealthy people are business owners, a part of German society known as the *Mittelstand*, a difficult-to-translate term referring to the mostly family-owned small and medium-sized enterprises that make up the bulk of the German economy. (Do not confuse *Mittelstand* with *Mittelschicht*, the middle class, about two-thirds of Germany's 82 million population.) The *Mittelstand* in turn is generally divided into two main categories: (1) "classic" German firms, with revenue below 50 million euros (99 percent of all firms), and (2) "upper-sized" firms, with revenue of 50 million up to 1 billion euros (0.34 percent). The remaining small percentage are large, better-known corporations, many listed in the DAX 30 index. But the "classic" and "upper-sized" firms together account for 68 percent of Germany's exports. The large enterprises (only 0.02 percent of the total) produce the remaining 32 percent of exports, and not all economists categorize them as part of the *Mittelstand*. There is also a debate in Germany over whether entrepreneurial startups and other newer forms of smaller, "solo self-employed" operations should be included in the *Mittelstand* category. Some of these firms do not meet the criterion of "ownership and management in one hand."

Germany has been slow to address the impact that German tax law has on income inequality. Generally, income tax provisions favor business owners and the *Mittelstand*. Despite recent court rulings that labeled the inheritance tax and other elements of taxation as disproportionately favoring businesses over individual taxpayers, little has changed. That is in part due to the fact that many Germans feel that business owners deserve tax breaks because they provide jobs. But the inheritance tax structure tends to keep wealth in the hands of *Mittelstand* companies and the families that run them.

Related Web link: bundesregierung.de—this main site of the German government offers information about German society (E, G)

Germany and the World Billionaires Count

According to the *Forbes* magazine annual list, there were 2,043 billionaires in the world at the end of 2017. (In fact, there is some disagreement over the exact total count of U.S. dollar billionaires, which varies according to who's counting. More about that below.) Which countries top the list?

Again, the ranking can vary by source, but in 2016 and 2017, the five countries with the most billionaires were: (1) United States, (2) China, (3) Germany, (4) India, and (5) Russia. If expanded to include UHNWIs (Ultra High Net Worth Individuals, above $30 million), the first three nations remain the same, but the United Kingdom takes the fourth spot, while France is fifth (Statista, 2016, 2017).

Now we come to those sources. Responding to the varying results from several different sources, the editors of *Private Banking* magazine decided to combine three different results and derive average figures out of that for the number and rank of billionaires in Germany. Using data from *Manager Magazin, Bilanz,* and *Forbes,* these were the results for 2016:

1. Herbert Quandt and family, including Susanne Quandt Klatten (Altana, SGL Carbon) and Stefan Quandt: €32.4 billion (BMW, Munich)

2. Henkel family, Hans Van Bylen (CEO), Simone Bagel Trah (Chair of the Supervisory Board, Düsseldorf): €26.8 billion (Henkel company, chemicals and consumer goods, Loctite)

3. Reimann family: Renate Reimann-Haas and Wolfgang Reimann; brothers Matthias Reimann-Andersen and Stefan Reimann-Andersen (Reckitt Benckiser, London and Ludwigshafen): €25.3 billion; related enterprises: JAB: Coty (perfumes, cosmetics), Keurig Green Mountain, Peets (coffee), Jacobs Douwe Egberts (coffee)

4. Schaeffler family: Maria Elisabeth Schaeffler-Thumann, Georg Friedrich Wilhelm Schaeffler: €22.8 billion (Schaeffler automotive, Herzogenaurach; Continental tires, 46 percent share)

5. Karl Albrecht Jr. and Beate Heister: €21.6 billion (Aldi Süd discount grocery stores, Essen-Schonnebeck)

6. Dieter Schwarz: €19.4 billion (Lidl & Schwarz; Lidl, Kaufland discount markets, Neckarsulm)

Germany's billionaires and most other wealthy Germans tend to keep a very low profile. It is difficult to find even a single public photograph of some of them. Austria's top billionaire (one of nine in Austria), Red Bull founder Dietrich "Didi" Mateschitz, worth $23.4 billion in 2017 (*Forbes*), may not be as well known as Jeff Bezos or Bill Gates, but he is less of a recluse than most of his German-speaking peers. He has been known to appear at some Red Bull public events.

Where in Germany do you find the most multimillionaires and billionaires? The top ten cities for UHNWIs are:

1.	Hamburg:	95
2.	Munich (München):	62
3.	Düsseldorf	30
4.	Berlin	29
5.	Stuttgart	19
6.	Cologne (Köln)	16
7.	Bremen/Bremerhaven	14
8.	Frankfurt am Main	12
9.	Essen	11
10.	Bielefeld	9

Sources: *Statista, UBS, Wealth-X, and World Wealth Report (WWR)*

German Citizenship: *Jus Soli Versus Jus Sanguinis*

The world is generally divided into those countries that determine citizenship based on where a person is born (*jus soli*, Latin for "law of the soil"; *Bodenrecht* in German) and those that determine citizenship based on parentage (*jus sanguinis*, Latin for "law of blood"; *Blutsrecht* in German). Germany is among those nations that have citizenship laws based on the latter.

Except for minor amendments, Germany's existing *jus sanguinis* citizenship laws date back to 1914 and a time when the population was much more homogeneous and relatively free of *Ausländer* (foreigners). The *Blutsrecht* principle itself actually goes back to Bavaria in 1818 and went into effect in the German Reich in 1870.

Today's much more "*multi-kulti*" Germany finds itself clashing with the contradictions and inequities that *Blutsrecht* causes in a country that is now home to more than 7 million *Ausländer*, nearly 9 percent of Germany's total population of 82 million. Few of these 7 million permanent residents have German citizenship. The fact that almost one in four of these "foreigners" was born in Germany and acts and talks like any other German has not yet helped them become German citizens. Germany's 3 million Turks, the largest foreign contingent, have long felt discriminated against by the naturalization hurdle.

While a foreigner living in France or Great Britain can apply for citizenship after only 5 years of residence, Germany used to make its foreign nationals wait 15 long years (8 years for children age 16 to 23). Of the 15 EU countries, Germany stood with Austria, Luxembourg, Spain, and Sweden as the only countries that did not grant automatic citizenship to children born in the country. The other 10 not only do so but also allow dual citizenship.

Critics of the strict naturalization laws viewed them as a relic of the past that was preventing the integration and full participation of Germany's foreign citizens. Change came when Gerhard Schröder became chancellor in late 1998. Schröder and his SPD/Green coalition government pushed through more liberal naturalization laws, including dual citizenship, despite the opposition of the CDU/CSU party.

Highlights of Germany's New Citizenship Law

- The time required before a foreigner can apply for citizenship, formerly 15 years, is now 8 years.
- A foreign spouse of a German citizen can apply for citizenship after only 3 years.
- Any child born in Germany automatically becomes a German citizen as long as at least one parent was also born in Germany.
- Foreigners may obtain German citizenship and retain their former citizenship.
- Naturalized citizens must demonstrate that they can speak German and pledge to uphold the German constitution and the democratic system.
- New citizens must prove they have no criminal record, can financially support themselves, and are not likely to end up on welfare assistance.

Migrant and Minority Issues: *Migrations-hintergrund* (Migrant Background)

Germany's minority population has grown dramatically since 2001, but especially over the past decade. This increase is due in large part to the many asylum-seekers who fled to Europe and Germany to escape war and poverty, but that was not the only factor. Half of the 18.6 million "foreigners" now living in Germany have German citizenship.

Germany began to track its non-German ethnic population only in 2005. In the official vernacular of German bureaucracy, *eine Person mit Migrationshintergrund* is a person living in Germany who was either not born there, or has at least one parent not born in Germany. The annual "microcensus" (*Mikrozensus*) is actually a type of statistical sampling of 1 percent of all households, rather than a true census (*Volkszählung*). The figures below refer to the 2016 micro-census unless noted otherwise.

Foreigners and ethnic minorities now make up 22.5 percent of Germany's total population of 82.8 million, up from just 9 percent in 2000. People of Turkish heritage number 3 million, by far the largest segment, and 2.3 million people have their roots in the Middle East, an increase of almost 51 percent since 2011. The number of people of African origin in Germany has nearly doubled in only 5 years, to 740,000.

While ethnic minorities are now over a fifth of Germany's population, they make up only 8 percent of the representatives in the Bundestag, Germany's parliament. Out of 58 migrant-background members of parliament, only 11 have Turkish roots, and one is Afro-German.

The most prominent politician of Turkish heritage, Cem Özdemir, first entered the Bundestag in 1994. Born in Swabia, Özdemir has served as cochair of the Green party since 2008. He has long fought to see Turkish-Germans and other minorities be better accepted in German society. The recent rise of the right-wing, anti-immigrant AfD party in the Bundestag since 2017 has not made that task any easier.

In 2013 Karamba Diaby (SPD) and Charles M. Huber (CDU) became the first Afro-Germans ever to be elected to the Bundestag. Both have roots in Senegal. During his successful 2017 reelection campaign, Diaby faced a hateful torrent of online abuse in the eastern state of Saxony-Anhalt, a hotbed of anti-foreigner sentiment. Huber decided not to run again in 2017, citing a lack of support from the Darmstadt CDU.

A recent study proved what many already knew: If you don't look or sound "German" in Germany, you can face verbal abuse, discrimination, racial profiling, and worse. Tahir Della, a Berlin-based spokesman for *Initiative Schwarze Menschen in Deutschland*, a nongovernmental organization that defends the rights of people of color, says the authorities "have absolutely no idea" that what they're doing is racist. Racial profiling in Germany is a "societal, structural problem" that isn't being discussed, he added.

Behinderte: Germans with Disabilities

Any truly organized movement aimed at fighting discrimination against and obtaining improved rights for people with disabilities has been slow to evolve in Germany. In the 1960s, such activities were mostly limited to the field of sports. In the 1970s, according to Germany's Association for Independent Living (ISL), the movement began to take on an increasingly political character and to deal with larger, more general issues concerning people with disabilities. The first tentative steps toward setting up an organization for those purposes were taken at the so-called *Krüppeltribunal* (cripples' tribunal) in 1981 in Düsseldorf. After that first meeting of disabled persons from all over Germany, another five years went by before the actual establishment of the first Zentrum für Selbstbestimmtes Leben (Center for Independent Living) in Bremen.

Critics of Germany's slow progress in the area of improved conditions for people with disabilities point to laws in Sweden, the United States, Canada, and other countries that have greatly enhanced accessibility to buildings, public transportation, and cultural events, and they ask why Germany has been reluctant to pass similar laws. Although there are many international and European recommendations for easier access, these critics say, Germany and some other European countries have failed to take the needed steps to make them a reality.

While some advancement has taken place in the last decade, many German apartment buildings, even those with four or five floors, have no elevator. Only recently did the German railway Deutsche Bahn move to provide wheelchair access in its trains.

Germany's organizations representing disabled persons are trying to persuade German legislators to pass laws that would not only require easy access to buildings but also encourage better social integration and equality for people with special needs and make it possible for them to live more independent lives.

Related Web links: **behinderung.org**—information and help for disabled people in Germany (G); **handicap-info.de**—one of the best German sites for issues concerning the disabled (G); **isl-ev.de**—Interessenvertretung Selbstbestimmt Leben, a German organization aimed at better independent living for people with disabilities (G); **dpi.org**—DPI, Disabled Peoples' International (E); **sath.org**—Society for Accessible Travel and Hospitality (U.S.) (E); **gimponthego.com**—Gimp on the Go, international accessibility for travelers with disabilities (E)

Sex und Sitten (Sex and Morals)

Probably the single most important aspect that sets German and European social and sexual mores apart from those in the English-speaking world is the lack of any Puritan past. A glance through almost any mainstream German magazine, with its casual display of photos of naked or semi-naked women, graphically illustrates that point. Even some German newspapers have the standard page-two topless photo every day—a practice that would raise eyebrows in Iowa but doesn't cause so much as a nod in Niedersachsen.

Despite their casual attitude about nudity, Germans have never been counted among the world's great lovers. Casanova (1725–98) was Italian; Don Juan was a legendary Spaniard. Germans, rightly or wrongly, are not noted for being passionate paramours. Although Germans like to think of themselves as romantics, it is only in a dreamy, more intellectual sense. (*Die Romantik* was a German literary epoch around the beginning of the 19th century.) A German's idea of "romantic" is a trip to Italy.

Sex, however, is another matter. Almost any German town of average size has its designated red-light district, where regulated houses of prostitution can be found. This phenomenon is most apparent in Hamburg's notorious *Reeperbahn* "entertainment" district, or at nightfall in certain sections of Berlin's Mitte district, where throngs of streetwalkers (*Straßenstrich*, *Autostrich*) often cause minor traffic jams. Even smaller German towns often have a designated *Dirnenviertel* or *Rotlichtrevier* (red-light district) with so-called Eros-Centers (formerly called *Bordelle* or *Freudenhäuser*), and *Call-girl* is now a German word. Under German as well as most other Western European law, prostitution, both heterosexual and homosexual, is for the most part not a punishable offense, and the trade is regulated for health reasons. In its refusal to close down a hooker (*Nutten*) operation associated with a Berlin bar, a German court also declared that prostitution was no longer considered *Sittenwidrig* (immoral, illegal). However, the Netherlands, not Germany, is the only European country that has actually fully legalized prostitution.

Yet, in spite of the court's claim and the efforts of Beate Uhse (1919–2001), Germany's most famous promoter of sexual liberation (and owner of a large chain of sex shops), the sex industry in general continues to be plagued by double standards, a sleazy image, and criminal elements—in Germany as elsewhere. Since the 1970s, prostitutes in France, Germany, the Netherlands, and a few other European countries have formed their own associations or unions. In Germany, a prostitute's income (*Dirnenlohn*) is legally subject to income taxes and a law that went into effect in 2002 made prostitutes eligible for health and retirement benefits.

Related Web links: beateuhse.de—Beate Uhse (adult content) (E, G); fau.org—a German prostitutes union site (E, G)

Marriage Equality in Germany: *"Ehe für alle"*

It's somewhat baffling why it took so long for Germany to legally recognize *Ehe für alle* ("Marriage for all"). Although German (Prussian, Nazi) law traditionally took a punitive approach toward homosexuals (see p. 122), these days a gay or lesbian lifestyle is widely accepted in Germany, with most of the population feeling that sexual orientation is a non-issue. An openly gay man, Klaus Wowereit, served as Berlin's mayor from 2001 to 2014. But in terms of legislation, until very recently, Germany lagged behind many other European nations in LGBTQ rights. The Netherlands (2001), Belgium (2003), Spain (2005), Sweden (2009), and several other countries fully legalized same-sex marriage years before Germany, which came rather late to the game.

Germany did not grant gay and lesbian partners even some of the legal rights enjoyed by married heterosexual couples until 2001, when it approved "registered life partnerships" (*Eingetragene Lebenspartnerschaft*). Although polls indicated that about 83 percent of Germans supported it, same-sex marriage was long opposed by Germany's ruling political parties. In particular, the dual "Christian" conservative parties, the Christian Democratic Union (CDU), led by chancellor Angela Merkel, and its Bavarian partner party, the Christian Socialist Union (CSU), stubbornly opposed full marriage equality for homosexual couples.

On June 30, 2017, Germany became the 14th European country to legalize gay marriage, and the 23rd worldwide, following a historic Bundestag vote. Chancellor Merkel, after a surprising change of heart, agreed to a proposal put forward by the Social Democratic (SPD) party to hold a vote on marriage equality. In the end, the vote was 393 to 226 in favor (with four abstentions). The chancellor, the daughter of a Protestant minister, still cast a "no" vote.

It would be October 1, 2017, before the first official same-sex nuptials could take place. Karl Kreile and Bodo Mende had the honor of being the first gay couple to tie the knot in Germany, appropriately in Berlin's Schöneberg district, known for its free-spirited gay and lesbian cultural history. The colorful, festive civil ceremony was held in Schöneberg's town hall, and the couple, who had lived together for 38 years, were honored to be the first to break the marriage equality barrier and no longer feel like "second-class citizens."

But there was one final hurdle the newlyweds had to face. German efficiency took another hit when their union could not be entered officially in the electronic marriage register. That couldn't happen until the software was updated to allow for two entries with the same sex.

Gays and Lesbians in Germany: Pink Triangles and Paragraph 175

Widely considered the "father of the gay rights movement," the German physician Dr. Magnus Hirschfeld (1868–1935) founded the Scientific Humanitarian Committee (das Wissenschaftlich-humanitäre Komitee) in 1897. While urging public figures in Germany to openly support homosexual rights, Hirschfeld wrote that "the liberation of homosexuals can only be the work of homosexuals themselves." He believed homosexuality to be a natural, biological trait deserving scientific investigation rather than scorn. Hirschfeld, a *transvestite*, coined the term *transvestism* and published many volumes on the topic. He even played himself in the sex-information silent film *Different from the Others (Anders als die Anderen)* in 1919. That same year, he founded the Institute for Sexual Science in Berlin, which carried out research on "the third sex" and the causes of homosexuality. He brought the formerly taboo topic into public discussion and fought for the repeal of Germany's Paragraph 175, a law dating back to 1871 making sex between males a crime subject to imprisonment.

The rise of German fascism in the 1920s ushered in a much less enlightened attitude toward homosexuals. Hirschfeld, who was Jewish, was forced into exile in France in 1930, and his institute became a prime target of the book burning on Berlin's Opernplatz on May 10, 1933. While the Nazis forced Jews to wear yellow stars, homosexuals were put in concentration camps and wore pink triangles.

The Nazis made Paragraph 175 even more strict, partly in reaction to Berlin's wide-open gay and lesbian scene (*Schwulen- und Lesbenszene*) in the 1920s and early '30s. It is therefore ironic that a prominent Nazi, Ernst Röhm, the head of the SA (*Sturmabteilung—* storm troopers), was a known homosexual. His elimination on Hitler's orders in 1934 was probably more for political reasons, but the National Socialists persecuted gays throughout their 12-year reign.

Although gays and lesbians in Germany now enjoy more tolerant attitudes and certain legal protections, Paragraph 175 was not completely abolished until 1994. The German political scene in recent years has produced some successful openly gay candidates at the local and state levels, although German gay and lesbian groups are still confronting conservative politicians over various LGBTQ-related issues. Most larger German cities, led by Berlin (which had an openly gay mayor from 2001 to 2014), have thriving gay communities. Even Munich's Oktoberfest features the *Bräurosl* "gay day," and the city's gay radio station is called Uferlos, which means "boundless." It is noteworthy that Catholic Bavaria was free of the repressive antigay laws found in Protestant Prussia in the late 19th century.

Related Web links: lsvd.de—LSVD online, Lesben- und Schwulenverband in Deutschland (Lesbian and Gay Association in Germany) (G); huk.org—Homosexuelle und Kirche (Homosexuals and the Church Ecumenical Group) (adult content) (E, G); pink-triangle.org—Pink Triangle (adult content) (E); uferlos-magazin.de—Uferlos 92.4 FM radio (Munich)

Death in Deutschland

"Die Beschäftigung mit dem Tode ist die Wurzel der Kultur." ("Dealing with death is the root of culture.")

—FRIEDRICH DÜRRENMATT (1921–990), SWISS AUTHOR AND DRAMATIST

The German way of death may be even more regulated than the German way of life. The German propensity to regulate almost every aspect of daily life carries over into the afterlife, with Germany's funeral industry among the most regulated in the world.

Cremation (*Einäscherung, Feuerbestattung*) has become increasingly popular in Germany, but if you want to spread grandpa's ashes in the woods where he loved to hike, you should be aware that that is verboten in most of Germany's states. The funeral home (*Bestattungsinstitut*) or crematorium controls the distribution of the cremains, which first must be placed in an appropriate container, usually a metal urn. Only in some *Länder* are the survivors entitled to take possession of the urn, and even then its final destination may be dictated by law: cemetery burial, placement in a columbarium, or spreading of the ashes in an approved cemetery lawn or forest. *Friedhofszwang* means that even cremains must end up in a cemetery.

The rules and regulations for normal burial are even more onerous and expensive. The costs for embalming, a nice coffin (required in most states), gravesite rental, etc. mean an average burial may run over 5,000 euros. Thus, Germany has seen a trend toward cremation and discount funerals.

In 1960, just over 10 percent of deceased Germans were cremated. By 1990, that rate was 23.7 percent, and that was the beginning of a dramatic increase in the cremation rate, which is now above 60 percent (2015). There are regional differences. In eastern Germany more than 80 percent opt for "ashes to ashes." But even in Catholic Bavaria the cremation rate has increased. Urban centers have higher cremation rates than rural areas.

The term "corpse tourism" refers to Germans avoiding the high costs and heavy-handed regulations at home by going to less regulated neighboring countries. The Swiss sections of Lake Constance are popular with Germans for spreading ashes, something illegal along the German shore. Cremation is cheaper in Poland and the Netherlands, even with shipping. German operators have responded by offering discount funeral services.

Even after someone lies legally and properly buried in one of Germany's 32,000 cemeteries, their resting place is only temporary. Germany has limited space for the 900,000 people who expire each year. A grave lease lasts an average of 23 years, although it may be extended if someone is willing to pay for it. When your time is up, your spot is turned over to some "body" else. Your bones or ashes are placed deeper or off to the side, and a new gravestone appears with a different name and dates.

Related Web links: postmortal.de—Der Tod in Deutschland (Death in Germany), a site devoted to changing Germany's overregulated funeral industry (G);

begraebnis.at—an Austrian funeral site with information about Austrian (Catholic) aspects of dealing with burials (G)

From Benz to Porsche

As Karl Benz drove his noisy, gasoline-powered, three-wheeled *Motorenwagen* through the streets of Mannheim in 1885, he could not have begun to imagine what an amazing impact his new invention would have on the world. About the same time, Gottlieb Daimler was working on a similar motorcar near Stuttgart. Although they lived only a few hundred miles apart, Daimler and Benz never met. The companies they each had formed were merged in 1926 to create the industrial giant known as Daimler-Benz AG until 1998. Seventy-two years after the first merger, a second created DaimlerChrysler AG by combining Daimler-Benz AG and America's Chrysler Motors, though this union ended in 2007, when Daimler AG divested Chrysler.

Neither Benz nor Daimler would have had an internal combustion engine to run the first *Motorenwagen* had not Nikolaus August Otto invented the gasoline-powered engine in 1861. Otto went on to develop the four-stroke engine in (1878) and founded his own company to manufacture engines.

Daimler and fellow engineer Wilhelm Maybach worked with Otto until they left to start their own company in 1882. Eight years later, Daimler founded the Daimler-Motoren-Gesellschaft, and around 1900, Maybach helped design the first Mercedes car, named for Daimler's daughter.

Germans still prefer to buy and drive the vehicles they are so good at manufacturing. Foreign automakers have a hard time in the German market, but German automakers such as Audi (VW), BMW, Daimler (Mercedes), Opel, Porsche, and Volkswagen are known worldwide.

The five Opel brothers began manufacturing bicycles in Rüsselsheim in 1886. Today the firm known as Adam Opel AG, now a division of France's Groupe PSA, is one of Germany's largest automakers. Volkswagen is Europe's largest automaker and one of the world's best-known auto brands. Stuttgart is home to two famous car brands: Mercedes (Daimler) and Porsche. The Bayrische Motorenwerke (BMW) calls Munich home.

Names Associated with the Automobile and Its Development

DEVELOPER	INVENTION/CONTRIBUTION
Karl Benz (1844–1929)	first practical automobile (1885)
Robert Bosch (1861–1942)	spark plug (1902); magneto
Gottlieb Daimler (1834–1900)	first motorcycle (1885); founded Daimler-Motoren-Gesellschaft (1890)
Rudolf Diesel (1858–1913)	diesel engine (1892)
Eugen Langen (1833–95)	worked with Nikolaus Otto; suspended monorail
Wilhelm Maybach (1864–1929)	design of the first Mercedes (1900–01)
Adam Opel (1837–95)	founded Adam Opel AG, now part of GM (1929–2017)
Nikolaus Otto (1832–91)	first gasoline engine (1861); four-stroke version (1878)
Ferdinand Porsche (1875–1951)	design of the first Volkswagen (1934)

Related Web links: **bmw.de**—BMW (E, G); **bosch.de**—
Bosch AG (G); **volkswagen.de**—Volkswagen AG (G);
daimler.com—Daimler (E)

At BMW World in Munich, new owners can pick up their brand new BMW car.

TRANSPORTATION
Driving in Deutschland

The $2,000 driver's license is only the beginning! Germans are crazy about their cars and take driving seriously. How seriously? Well, a German driver's license (*Führerschein*) costs $1,500 to $2,000 and requires a minimum of 25 to 45 hours of professional instruction plus 12 hours of theory. (The largest share of the expense comes from the fees for mandatory driving lessons. Thus are German parents spared the joys of teaching their offspring to drive.) It seemed like a better bargain when a German driver's license was valid for life. That changed in 2013 when, following EU guidelines, German licenses became valid for only 15 years. Licenses issued before January 19, 2013 will expire on January 19, 2033.

A non-German resident is allowed to drive for up to one year with a foreign license. If you are going to be living in Germany for more than one year, it is wise to begin the process of getting a German license after you have been in the country for six months, well in advance of the end of the one-year period. What you have to do to get your new *Führerschein* is largely a matter of geography, timing, luck, and money.

A foreign resident in Germany can usually acquire a German license for much less than a German starting out as a beginning driver—about $600 to $800. The cost comes in the form of paying for things like the following: an eye test (from a licensed optician, of course), a translation of your home license into German, fees (written exam, driving school lessons/test, certificates, and so forth), and the required first aid course.

If you are lucky, you will have a license from a country or one of the U.S. states with which Germany has a reciprocity agreement. That can help you avoid some of the hoops through which less fortunate folks have to jump—although they are largely the same hoops a German citizen confronts. To get a license, Germans 18 years of age or older must attend a driving school (*Fahrschule*) and take both a written and a practical test. The practical exam is thorough and includes driving in a variety of situations—city streets, autobahn, and so forth.

Studying the German traffic rules for the written exam is a good idea even if you don't have to take the exam. Germany and Europe have some rules of the road that differ significantly from American practice. Probably the most important difference is the right-priority rule. Unless signs indicate otherwise, vehicles coming from the right have the right-of-way. Also, since most German road signs are symbols, without words (*ohne Worte*), it is wise to learn to recognize the many signs that may not be familiar to a foreigner.

Related Web link: german-way.com—Search for "How to Get a German Driver's License" (E)

Flensburg and the KBA: Keeping Score on Germany's Drivers

The German city of Flensburg lies just a stein's throw from Denmark on the Flensburg Fjord. Situated almost as far north as one can go without leaving Germany, Flensburg is much more than just another place on the map for Germany's drivers, for it is in Flensburg that one finds the German institution known as the Kraftfahrt-Bundesamt (KBA), Germany's federal department of motor vehicles. Since 1974, the KBA has been responsible for keeping track of drivers' traffic violation points and maintaining a central registry for all of Germany: This also applies to tourists and foreigners driving in Germany.

When a driver is caught violating one of the provisions in Germany's *Straßenverkehrs-Ordnung* (StVO, "traffic regulations"), the police notify the KBA. The KBA in turn records and archives the number of points for each violation. A new penalty point system took effect in Germany on May 1, 2014. At that time any old penalty points a driver had were converted to the new system. Any driver who accumulates a total of 8 points automatically loses his or her license. A single serious violation can earn a driver 2 or 3 points. Drunken driving (*Trunkenheit am Steuer*), leaving the scene of an accident (*Verkehrsunfallflucht*), and driving in the wrong direction on the autobahn (*Fahren entgegen der Fahrtrichtung auf der Autobahn*) are all rated at 2-3 points each. Minor violations will earn a driver 1 point. More serious offenses, however, have various point values up to the maximum of 3. Running a red light, for example, will draw 2 points.

The Flensburg point system is rigid. Drivers can't even contest any of their points until after the license has been revoked. They also can't dispute the KBA's records. Points for minor violations last for 2.5 years. Points for more serious offenses stay in the Flensburg registry for 10 years.

Motorists can request their *Kontostand*, or account balance, from Flensburg in writing. Germany's privacy laws prohibit phone or email requests via the KBA's website. Under the new law, when drivers accumulate 4 to 5 points, they receive a warning, along with information about the points system. With 6 to 7 points, a driver must attend 2 90-minute seminars within 3 months. With 8 or more points, the driver's license is revoked. There is no longer any way to voluntarily reduce your traffic violation points. Note that in addition to points, moving violations can also result in fines of up to €1500 and the temporary or permanent revocation of your driver's license. A permanently revoked license can only be reinstated following an official psychological assessment, the so-called MPU (*Medizinisch-Psychologische Untersuchung*). Passing the MPU examination can be difficult.

Related Web links: kba.de—Kraftfahrt-Bundesamt Flensburg (Federal Motor Transport Authority), (E, G); **dvr.de**—Deutsche Verkehrssicherheitsrat (German Traffic Safety Organization) (G)

Public Transport

Although Germans are known for their love of the automobile and driving, Germany is a place where one can generally get around easily without a car. All German cities of average or larger size have extensive, well-used public transportation systems consisting of a mix of buses, streetcars, and commuter rail lines. Berlin, Frankfurt am Main, Hamburg, Stuttgart, and Munich all have metro systems that run above and below ground. The German underground metros are referred as the U-Bahn, while the above-ground commuter rail lines are known as the S-Bahn. Soon you will learn that the U-Bahn sometimes runs above ground, while there are also subterranean S-Bahn lines.

S-Bahn stations are marked with a white S on a green circle. U-Bahn stations are indicated by a white U on a blue circle. Bus and tram stops are marked with a large *H* on a yellow circular sign. Both the S-Bahn and U-Bahn use an open-entry system without turnstyles or ticket collectors. On buses and streetcars you can buy a ticket from the driver or an onboard ticket machine. S-Bahn and U-Bahn tickets must be purchased in advance. You can save money by buying special all-day, weekly, monthly, student, senior, or multiple tickets (*Streifenkarten/Sammelkarten*, a strip of four to seven tickets). Unless you have a long-term pass, you must also validate your ticket by using a red or yellow *Entwerter* that is located on the platform of the S-Bahn and U-Bahn or inside the bus or tram (In Hamburg and some cities, you can't buy a ticket in advance, so you don't need to validate it.). You are not even supposed to be on the platform without a valid ticket, but under Germany's honor system, no one will check. However, occasional sting operations on the S-Bahn and U-Bahn catch and fine passengers who haven't been completely "honorable."

In Frankfurt and Munich, the S-Bahn also conveniently links downtown (*die City*) and the airport (*der Flughafen*). In Frankfurt, it takes a mere 12 minutes to make the trip. In Munich, you should allow about 45 minutes.

Related Web links: Public transportation authorities: **bvg.de**—BVG, Berlin (E, G); **hvv.de**—HVV, Hamburg (G); **vrr.de**—Verkehrsverbund Rhein-Ruhr, Düsseldorf/Dortmund region (G); **vvs.de**—VVS, Stuttgart (G); **mvv-muenchen .de**—MVV, Munich (G); **vrsinfo.de**—Verkehrsverbund Rhein-Sieg, Cologne/Bonn region (G); **rmv.de**—Rhein-Main Verkehrsverbund, Frankfurt region (G); **vrn.de**—Verkehrsverbund Rhein-Neckar, Mannheim region (G); **vbn.de**—Verkehrsverbund Bremen/Niedersachsen, Bremen region (G); **evag.de**—EVAG, Essen (G)

Riding the German Rails

Traveling by train in Europe can be a lot more pleasant if you know a few tricks of the trade. Because all large to medium-size cities, as well as many smaller communities, in German-speaking Europe have a train station (or two or three), train travel is convenient and efficient, although increasingly expensive. The main train station (*Hauptbahnhof*) is usually in the center of town, from which commuter trains, taxis, streetcars, and buses can take the traveler straight to a local destination. The weakest link in this otherwise efficient chain is often the Deutsche Bahn ticket office at the station, where it seems there are always too few ticket agents. Long lines and long waits are all too common, but DB has improved its ticket sales service in recent years.

The privatized Deutsche Bahn AG (DB) finally entered the modern financial era in 1992 by accepting credit cards. However, it has taken many years to get to the point where customers can use a credit card at any DB ticket counter without any problems. Paying for tickets online with a credit card is still problematic, although EC bank card payment works well. Although many Germans today use a barcode on their smartphone as a ticket, that doesn't help foreign tourists who want to pay for a German train ticket with a credit card online. Usually it's simpler to go to the nearest train station and buy your ticket in person using cash or a credit card.

If you'll be residing in Germany for a long time, it may be a good idea to get a Bahncard. This DB discount card also functions as a Visa credit card (since 2013). There are several different versions of the Bahncard, but they all offer a way to buy DB tickets at up to a 50 percent discount. The Bahncard 100 allows you to travel by rail at no further cost. Bahncards are issued in first-class and second-class versions. If you travel frequently by rail in Germany, a Bahncard is a good idea. Over 5 million Germans have one.

European trains are divided into first and second class. Look for a large "1" or "2" painted on the car near the door. In general, first-class rail travel costs about double the second-class rate, but that is not always the case. Sometimes a first-class ticket is only about 30 percent more than a second-class ticket. It pays to compare the two prices for any particular trip.

You can use the practical *Wagenstandanzeiger* (car locator, also called the *Wagenreihungsplan*) to find your train car on the long rail platform and avoid walking through half the train to find your seat. The platform is divided into sections labeled "A" to "E." The car locator can tell you almost to the nearest meter where your car will stop. Find the car number on your ticket and use the graphic guide located on the platform to see exactly where your car will be.

Related Web links: **bahn.de**—Deutsche Bahn AG, a good site that also offers online ticket purchasing (E, G); **bahn.com/en/view/offers/bahncard/bahncard.shtml** —Bahncard info in English; **reiseauskunft.bahn.de**— Deutsche Bahn's online rail ticket and schedule information (E, G); **eurail.com**—Eurail (E); **dbmuseum.de**—Deutsche Bahn Museum—this rail transportation museum is located in Nuremberg (E, G); **sbb.ch**—SBB Online, Swiss railroad (E, G); **oebb.at**—ÖBB, Austrian railway (G)

TRANSPORTATION
Der Liegewagen Versus the ICE

Some rail travel enthusiasts have come to appreciate *couchette* travel, while others use it only as a last resort or never. Offered by most European railways, a *couchette* car (*Liegewagen*) features compartments that have regular seats by day and sleeping bunks by night. Such *Nachtzüge* (night trains) are usually scheduled to leave in the late afternoon and arrive in the morning. (More expensive Pullman/*Schlafwagen* accommodations are also available on *Nachtzüge*.) Intended for longer overnight journeys such as Berlin–Paris or Hamburg–Munich, the *couchette* seats on each side of the compartment magically transform into four or six bunks. The porter drops off a blanket, a pillow, and a pocketlike sheet for each person. After some clever unfolding and the snapping of a few latches, the bunks are ready. There is no real privacy, and you probably won't know most of the people in the compartment. Your traveling companions may be male or female, young or old, and from any part of the world. *Couchette* travel is not for timid souls. It can be a fascinating adventure, a sleepless night, or both. You must make reservations for a *Liegewagen*, and there is a per-person *couchette* surcharge.

The increasing use of high-speed trains such as the German ICE (InterCityExpress) and the French TGV has reduced the need for overnight *couchette* travel in Germany and Europe. Deutsche Bahn (then still the old Bundesbahn) put its first ICE trains into service in 1991. Since then, several newer generations of the ICE have evolved. Today's German ICE can whisk you between Hamburg in the north and Munich in the south in less than six hours. In March 2018, a new ICE Sprinter route between Berlin and Munich reduced the travel time to just under 4 hours, cutting about 2 hours off the previous time and competing favorably with air travel.

The sleekly styled ICE 3 that began service in 2000 can reach a top speed of 330 kilometers (205 miles) per hour and, like all other ICEs, offers a quiet, jetliner-like interior (but roomier than a jet) with comfortable seats, free Wi-Fi, and power outlets. Because of their high speed, ICE cars are pressurized as well as air-conditioned. The ICE T is a "leaning" train that runs faster on regular lines not designed for the standard ICEs. The latest ICE model, the ICE 4, began regular service on some high-speed routes in December 2017. Deutsche Bahn plans to expand its ICE 4 fleet in coming years, offering top speeds of 230-250 km/h (143-155 mph).

Related Web links: bahn.de—Deutsche Bahn AG, search "CityNightLine" or "Nachtzug" (E, G); raileurope.com—booking site for ICE (E)

Europe—especially Germany and France—has seen an increase in the use of high-speed trains.

Schwarzfahrer: Don't Forget That Ticket!

Germany's extensive public transportation network functions for the most part on an honor system. Unlike subway or metro systems in most other countries, the commuter rail system in large and medium-size German cities and in Vienna has no tollgates or other barriers in S-Bahn (urban commuter line) or U-Bahn (underground/subway) stations. Since there are also no conductors on these conveyances, passengers are expected to have a valid ticket or pass in their possession before boarding a streetcar, train, or bus.

On average, fewer than 4 percent of Germany's daily commuters try to travel without a valid ticket. However, in certain areas and certain stations, the rate can be as high as 10 percent. In a recent crackdown over a period of six months by Hamburg's HVV public transportation authority, 150,000 fare dodgers (*Schwarzfahrer*) had to pay a 60 euro ($74) fine for not having a ticket. That was 3.6 percent of the total 4.2 million passengers that HVV checked. The current fine for traveling on public transport without a ticket (since 2015) is 60 euros nationwide in Germany.

Following its expansion after reunification, Berlin's metro system (BVG) has considered introducing a tollgate system with magnetic-striped tickets similar to that found in London, New York, and Paris. The hitch is that installing such a system in every S-Bahn or U-Bahn station would be an expensive way to combat increasing numbers of *Schwarzfahrer* in the German capital.

Although in most German-speaking cities, you can buy a ticket from a bus driver or a streetcar vending machine, it is cheaper to buy a *Sammelkarte* or *Streifenkarte*, offering several tickets together at a discount. There are usually also special tickets or passes for the day, week, or month, as well as discounted student and senior tickets. At many locations, you will find automatic ticket machines (*Fahrkartenautomaten*). Larger stations generally have a ticket booth where you can purchase any kind of ticket. Once you have a ticket, it is good on all buses, streetcars, and S-Bahn and U-Bahn trains within a city's network. Just don't forget to validate your ticket in the *Entwerter* or *Entgelter* located either at stations or inside buses and streetcars. An unstamped ticket is the same as no ticket. In Hamburg and some other cities, you can't buy a ticket in advance, so you don't need to validate it.

Related Web links: **bahn.de**—Deutsche Bahn AG, German rail (E, G); **bvg.de**—Berlin's public transportation authority (E, G); **hvv.de**—Hamburg's public transportation authority (E, G); **mvv-muenchen.de**—Munich's MVV transport agency (E, G)

Automatic ticket machines are found at many locations.

Germany's "Greyhound" Bus Revolution: FlixBus

Many Germans of a certain age had their first long-distance bus ride on a Greyhound or Trailways bus in the United States during an exchange visit or a vacation trip. A motor coach ride in Europe usually meant a chartered tour bus. But, as bus travel in North America has been declining, it has been booming in Europe, especially in Germany since 2013.

Before then, long-distance, intercity motor coach service in Germany was banned, with few exceptions. Long-distance bus travel was permitted only between countries in the European Union, but not within Germany. That all changed when German transport law was liberalized at the end of 2012. Although Germany has long had an excellent rail network, lawmakers wanted to encourage the much lower fares possible with bus travel. To prevent competition with local public transportation (bus, rail), there is a restriction stating that passengers may not be transported by bus between two stops that are less than 50 km (31 miles) apart, or if the rail travel time between them is less than 1 hour.

Suddenly there were all kinds of bus operators named DeinBus, FlixBus, MeinFernbus, Megabus, and Postbus competing to transport passengers across Germany for far less than air or rail fares, and with perks such as roomy seats, free Wi-Fi, a smartphone booking app, power outlets for charging, a toilet, snacks, and drinks. New bus service between German cities mushroomed. Special €5 fares help lure new customers, although they are limited to only the first few purchasers.

Over time, the number of operators has dwindled, leaving FlixBus with a 93 percent share of the German market in 2017 after various mergers and buyouts. The company's bright, neon-green coaches have transported over 100 million passengers in Germany and 25 other countries since 2013. FlixBus claims it is now the preferred method of travel across the European Union for people 18 to 25 years of age. About 60 percent of its customers are female.

Originally founded in Munich in 2011 as GoBus by three young German partners, in 2013 the company began operating three daily intercity routes in Bavaria under the FlixBus brand. Today, the firm claims 250,000 daily connections to 1,400 destinations in 26 countries. Partnered with 250 regional and local bus operators, FlixBus operates as a franchise that manages the technology, ticketing, network planning, branding, marketing, and sales. It plans to enter the U.S. market in 2018.

FlixBus has not been without its critics. Among other things, they have pointed out relatively low driver pay and the company's tendency to drop unprofitable destinations with little or no warning. Despite being a virtual monopoly, FlixBus claims it has brought innovation and improvements, including lower travel costs, to the travel market in Germany and Europe.

In August 2017 FlixBus announced the introduction of its rail service: FlixTrain. With teaser fares as low as €9.99, FlixTrain opened its Berlin-Stuttgart line with stops in Hanover and Frankfurt am Main. See flixtrain.de for current information.

Related Web links: flixbus.com—booking site, route maps, and schedules for Flixbus (E)

Quizlink Answers

Do as the Germans Do
1. b, 2. c, 3. a, 4. c, 5. b, 6. c, 7. b, 8. a, 9. c, 10. b, 11. b, 12. a, 13. c, 14. b

Places
1. a, 2. a, 3. a, 4. a(i), b(iii), c(ii); 5. a; 6. b; 7. c, 8. a; 9. c, 10. c, 11. b, 12. a

People
1. b, 2. c, 3. b, 4. a, 5. b, 6. b, 7. b, 8. b, 9. a, 10. c, 11. a, 12. c, 13. b, 14. b

Organizations
1. b, 2. c, 3. c, 4. b, 5. c, 6. c, 7. c, 8. a

Time
1. c, 2. b, 3. b, 4. b, 5. a, 6. c, 7. c, 8. b, 9. a, 10. b, 11. c, 12. b, 13. b

Quantity
1. c, 2. b, 3. c, 4. c, 5. c, 6. c, 7. b, 8. c, 9. b

Connections
1. c, 2. b, 3. c, 4. b, 5. c, 6. c, 7. a, 8. a, 9. c, 10. c

What's That?
1. a, 2. b, 3. c, 4. a, 5. c, 6. a, 7. a

Laws and Regulations
1. c, 2. c, 3. b, 4. b, 5. a, 6. b, 7. b, 8. c, 9. c, 10. b, 11. b

Know What the Germans Know
1. c, 2. b, 3. b, 4. a, 5. b, 6. a, 7. b, 8. c, 9. c, 10. c, 11. b, 12. c, 13. c

Index

Abbreviations, 92
ABC Bücherdienst GmbH, 32
Acronyms, 92
Adam Opel AG, 124
Advent, 25
Alcoholic beverages, 34
Aldi, 16
Allhallowtide, 23
Allianz, 16
Alpine skiing, 65
Alps, the, 65
Amazon, 32, 49
Android Pay, 27, 33
Apotheke (pharmacy), 69, 109
Apple Pay, 27, 33
Architecture, 12–13
Arcor, 112
Armed forces, 98
Aspirin, 69, 109
AT&T, 33, 111
ATMs, 14, 33, 34
Automakers, 16, 124–125

Babbel, 17, 87
Bad Segeberg, 11
Baedeker travel guides, 60
BahnCard, 89, 129
BahnTower, 13
Bakeries, 53
Bank drafts, 32
Banks, 14
Barbara Branch custom, 24
Barbarazweig, 24, 25
Basic Law, 98
Bathrooms, 40–41
Bauhaus, 12–13
Bavaria, 55, 56, 59
Bayer & Co, 109
Bayrische Motorenwerke (BMW), 124
Beach baskets, 22
Beer, 34, 53, 55–56
Berlin, 17, 94
    crime in, 84
    fashion in, 39
    history of, 62–63, 96–97
    Jewish presence in, 107
    store hours, 29
Berlin Brandenburg Willy Brandt Airport (BER), 18
Berlin Fashion Week, 39
Berlin Wall, 62, 72, 76, 96, 104
Bertelsmann, 16
Bibles, 105
Billionaires, 116
Birthdays, 19
Blue-collar workers, 37
Blu-ray, 49
BMW (Bayrische Motorenwerke), 124
BMW World, 125
Bonn, 96

Bonn/Berlin Law, 96
Boss, Hugo, 39
Boxing Day, 25
Brandenburg, 64
Brandenburg Gate, 97, 107
Brands, 16
Bread, 53–54
Bread & Butter, 39
Building projects, 18
Bundestag, 96, 99
Buses, 134
Business, 14–18

Candlemas, 20
Carnival season, 21
Celebrations. *see* Holidays and celebrations
Censorship, 93, 94
Central Council of Jews in Germany, 107
Childcare, 46
Christmas, 25
Church of Scientology, 108
Citizenship, 117
Class distinctions, 115–116
Clothes, 39
Consulate, 36
Conversation, 35
Conversion charts, 42–43
Corpse tourism, 123
Couchette car, 130
Craft beer, 55
Credit cards, 27, 33, 129
Cremation, 123
Crime, 84

Daily life, 33–43
    ATMs, 14, 33, 34
    bathrooms, 40–41
    clothes, 39
    conversation, 35
    electricity, 33
    emergency assistance, 36
    formality, 37–38
    loud noise, 34
    post offices, 31
    pushy behavior, 34
    restaurants, 38, 57
    rules, following, 35
    shopping, 27–32, 33, 34, 69, 109, 129
    Sie and *du*, 35, 37–38
    telephones, 31, 33, 111–113
    television, 33, 93
    weights and measures, 42–43
Daimler-Benz AG, 124
DaimlerChrysler AG, 16, 124
Death, 123
Death, causes of, 66
Democracy, 72
Deutsche Bahn, 129, 130
Deutsche Bank, 16

INDEX

Deutsche Telekom AG, 31, 112
Disabilities, people with, 119
Disney, 30, 48
Doors and locks, 83
Driving, 22, 126, 127
Drugstores, 69
DVDs, 49

East Germany. *see* German Democratic Republic
eBay, 17
E-commerce, 32
Economy, 14–18
Education, 44–47
Efficiency, 18
Elbe Philharmonic Hall, 18
Electricity, 33
Embassy, 36
Emergency assistance, 36
Entertainment, 48–51
   movies, 48, 49–50, 94
   music, 51
   television, 33, 93
Epiphany, 25
Euro, 15
European Central Bank, 15

The Factory, 17
Fashion, 39
Father Christmas, 25
Federal police, 86
Federal Republic of Germany, 59, 72, 85, 96, 98
Fiat Chrysler Automobiles, 16
Film production, 49
Films, 48, 49–50, 94
Flensburg, 127
FlixBus, 134
Food and drink, 52–58
   beer, 53, 55–56
   bread and sausage, 53–54
   restaurants, 38, 57
   sausage, 59
   water, 57, 58
   wine, 52
Foreign transaction fee, 33
Formality, 37–38
Frankfurt, 84
Fräulein and *Frau*, 38
Freedom House, 95
Friedrichstraße Station, 63
Funeral industry, 123

Garbage collection, 80
Garbage disposals, 78
Garden gnomes, 82
Gays and lesbians, 121–122
Geography, 59–65
German citizenship, 117
German Democratic Republic, 59, 72, 76, 98, 103, 104

German ICE, 130
German Institute for Jewish Studies, 107
German Unification Treaty, 96
German Unity Day, 72
German Wine Road, 82
Globe Theatre replica, 10
Google, 17
Groß-Friedrichsburg, 64
Groundhog Day, 20
GSM wireless standard, 33
Guest workers, 106

Halloween, 23
Hamburg, 18, 23
Das Handy, 31, 89, 111
HAQ Index, 66
Health and fitness, 66–69
Health insurance, 66
Healthcare system, 66
HelloFresh, 17
Higher education, 47
High-speed trains (ICE), 130–131
Holidays and celebrations, 18–26
   birthdays, 19
   Christmas and Advent, 25
   fifth season, 21
   Groundhog Day, 20
   Halloween, 23
   New Year's Eve, 26
   Saint Barbara's Day, 24
   summer vacation, 22
Holtzbrinck Publishing Group, 16
House and home, 77–83
   doors and locks, 83
   garbage collection, 80
   garden gnomes, 82
   home ownership, 77
   kitchens, 78
   loud noise, 34
   sweep week, 81
   washing machines, 79
House of Rothschild, 14
Humor, 35

Imperial Motion Picture Law, 94
Incarceration rates, 84
Income inequality, 115
Infant mortality rate, 66
Institute for Sexual Science, 122
InterCity Express (ICE), 89
Internet companies, 17
Internet usage, 111, 114
Interspar, 30
iPhone, 111

Jacobs University Bremen, 47
Jehovah's Witnesses, 108

Jewish Museum, 107
Jews, 103, 104, 107
Ketchup, 57
Kilometers vs. miles, 42, 43
Kindergarten, 44, 46
Kita, 46
Kitchens, 78
Kraftfahrt-Bundesamt (KBA), 127
Krampus, 25
Kreislaufstörung, 67
Lager, 55
Language, 87–92
    abbreviations and acronyms, 92
    in advertising, 89
    bathroom vs. toilet, 40
    Bible translations, 105
    borrowing, 91
    English invasion of, 89, 91
    false friends, 88
    in films, 49
    formality, 37–38
    Fräulein and Frau, 38
    learning, 87
    music, 51
    Sie and du, 35, 37–38
    spelling reform, 90
Language dilution, 89
Language exchanges, 87
Law enforcement, 84–86
    federal police, 86
    police forces, 85–86
Lidl, 16
Life expectancy, 66
Lines, standing in, 34
Loud noise, 34
Lutheran churches, 103, 104

Magazines, 95, 120
Map, 136
Mardi Gras, 21
Marriage equality, 121
Martinstag, 23
McDonald's, 34
Media, 93–95
Memorial to the Murdered Jews of Europe, 107
Mercedes, 124
Mercedes Benz Fashion Week, 39
Metric system, 42
Microsoft, 17
Miele, 79
Migrant issues, 118
Miles vs. kilometers, 42, 43
Mineral baths, 67
Mineral water, 58
Minority issues, 118
Mobile payment, 27, 33
Mobile phones, 31, 33, 111

Money
    ATMs, 14, 33, 34
    credit cards, 27, 33, 129
    the euro, 15
    mobile payment, 27, 33
Mosques, 106
Mountains, 65
Movies, 48, 49–50, 94
Multinational corporations, 16
Munich, 56, 77
Murder rate, 84
Music, 51
Muslims, 103, 104, 106

NATO (North Atlantic Treaty Organization), 98
Nazi era, 72, 85, 96, 98, 107, 122
Netflix, 49
Neuss, 10
New Year's Eve, 26
Newspapers, 95, 120
Nikolaustag, 25
Noise prevention, 34

Online banking, 14

Paragraph 175, 122
Pay phones, 112, 113
Paying in restaurants, 57
Poison control, 36
Police colors, 85
Police forces, 85–86
Political coalitions, 102
Political parties, 99, 100
Politics, 96–102
Porsche, 124
Post offices, 31
Prescription medication, 69
Press, 95
Privacy, 83
Private language schools, 87
Prostitution, 120
Protestants, 103, 104, 105
Pseudo-English terms, 91
Public broadcasting corporations, 93
Public transportation, 130–134

Queues, 34

Radio, 93
Reformationstag, 23
Reichstag, 62, 73, 96, 101
Religion, 103–108
    Bibles, 105
    church and state, 104
    Jews, 103, 104, 107
    Muslims, 103, 104, 106
    Protestants, 103, 104, 105
    Roman Catholic Church, 103, 104, 105
    Scientology, 108

INDEX

Restaurants, 38, 57
Restrooms, 40–41, 89
Roman Catholic Church, 103, 104, 105
Rules, following, 35
Rules, seven, 35

Saint Swithin's Day, 20
Samsung Pay, 27
SAP, 17
Sausage, 53–54, 59
S-Bahn, 128, 132
School choice, 45
Schools, 44, 45, 46
Science and technology
    aspirin, 69, 109
    Internet and tech startups, 17
    Internet usage, 111, 114
    space exploration, 110
    telecoms, 112
    telephones, 31, 33, 111–113
Scientology, 108
Sex, 120
Shopping, 27–32
    Apotheke (pharmacy), 69, 109
    bags, 34
    credit cards, 27, 33, 129
    e-commerce, 32
    online, 32
    post offices, 31
    store hours, 28–29
    Walmart, 30
Sie and *du*, 35, 37–38
Silicon Allee, 17
Ski resorts, 65
Skiing, 65
Skype, 17, 87
Smartphones, 111. *see also* Mobile phones
Smiling, 35
Smoking, 68
Social issues, 115–123
    billionaires, 116
    class distinctions, 115
    death and funeral industry, 123
    gays and lesbians, 121–122
    German citizenship, 117
    marriage equality, 121
    migrant and minority issues, 118
    Muslims, 103, 106
    people with disabilities, 119
    sex, 120
Sony Center, 13
Space exploration, 110
Sparkasse, 27
Spas, 67
Spätis, 29
Spelling reform, 90

St. Martin's Day, 23
St. Nicholas Day, 25
Store hours, 28–29
Stuttgart, 81
Stuttgart 21 (S21), 18
Summer vacation, 22
Swabia, 81
Sweep week, 81

TAN (transaction authentication number), 14
Tech startups, 17
Technology. *see* Science and technology
Telecoms, 112
Telekom Deutschland GmbH, 112
Telephones, 31, 33, 111–113
Television, 33, 93
Temperature, 42
Tipping, 57
T-Mobile, 33, 111
Traffic-light coalitions, 102
Trains, 129–133
Transportation, 124–134
    automakers, 16, 124–125
    buses, 134
    driving, 22, 126, 127
    public, 128, 129–133
    trains, 129–133
Transvestism, 122

U-Bahn, 128, 132
Ulfilas, 103, 105
Universities, 47

Video streaming, 49
Volkshochschule (VHS), 87

Waitresses, 38
Walmart, 30
Washing machines, 79
Water, 57, 58
Wealth, 115–116
Weights and measures, 42–43
Wertkauf, 30
West Germany. *see* Federal Republic of Germany
White-collar workers, 37
Wine, 34, 52
Witten/Herdecke University, 47
Women
    famous, 39, 71
    waitresses, 38

Yabla, 87

Zodiac signs, 19
Zoo Palast, 50